Wordly Wise

Kenneth Hodkinson

BOOK 5

Educators Publishing Service, Inc.
Cambridge and Toronto

COVER DESIGN/HUGH PRICE

May 2000 Printing

Contents

Word List

(Numbers in parentheses refer to the Word List in which the word appears.)

ABATE (20)
abound (17)
abstain (13)
abysmal (23)
abyss (4)
acclaim (10)
adroit (21)
adulation (15)
affront (3)
aggravate (13)
aghast (20)
agitate (2)
allude (12)
alms (15)
alternate (7)
ambiguous (21)
amends (19)
annihilate (17)
anthology (14)
antiseptic (1)
apathy (19)
apprehensive (2)
aquatic (10)
ardor (23)
arduous (24)
arena (8)
ascertain (14)
asset (2)
astute (14)
atrocity (5)
aural (14)
authentic (12)
avalanche (13)
awe (21)
awkward (24)

BAN (15)
barrier (24)
baton (12)
belligerent (10)
bellow (22)
besiege (15)
bigamy (17)
billow (4)
blizzard (10)
bondage (10)

bustle (9)

CADET (23)
camouflage (2)
canter (2)
castigate (11)
chalet (24)
charlatan (22)
chassis (6)
chronic (7)
clarity (12)
clergy (20)
clerical (16)
cockade (12)
cogitate (16)
coherent (1)
collaborate (13)
colossal (21)
commandeer (22)
compensate (7)
complicated (11)
concise (8)
conclude (22)
concur (21)
confer (3)
consider (17)
contemporary (6)
contempt (16)
corroborate (21)
create (11)
creditor (13)
crucial (14)
curb (23)

DAMASK (20)
deliberate (1)
denounce (23)
deplore (18)
deprive (4)
desolate (21)
despot (5)
determine (8)
devoid (24)
devoted (23)
devour (22)
dialect (17)

diehard (5)
dilatory (19)
dire (11)
discomfited (21)
discretion (18)
disfigured (23)
disgruntled (24)
disrupt (12)
doff (19)
doggerel (11)
dolt (1)
donate (9)
dub (18)
dubious (24)

EARMARK (22)
economical (19)
edible (23)
edit (15)
eerie (3)
effective (11)
elapse (1)
eliminate (12)
elope (17)
embalm (15)
embezzle (2)
emboss (14)
endeavor (22)
enthrall (7)
entrails (6)
envisage (24)
episode (19)
epitaph (21)
epoch (6)
equestrian (14)
equine (2)
erase (23)
erudite (20)
escapade (15)
espionage (14)
estuary (8)
exaggerate (13)
excel (4)
exceptional (11)
execute (21)
exemplary (1)

exert (24)
expansive (17)
expletive (11)
expose (13)
extensive (10)
extraordinary (3)

FACADE (20)
fateful (13)
felon (7)
ferment (20)
ferret (2)
fervor (3)
festive (23)
festoon (15)
fictitious (22)
financial (9)
fitful (19)
flippant (10)
floe (3)
fluctuate (11)
forbearance (14)
foreshadow (23)
forge (15)
fume (13)

GAVEL (22)
glib (20)
glower (2)
gnome (11)
gratitude (1)
groom (19)

HABITUAL (3)
halter (10)
hamper (19)
handicap (14)
hireling (12)
hovel (6)
hurtle (6)

ILLUSTRIOUS (9)
immerse (4)
impair (9)
impasse (13)
impertinent (16)

impound (18)
improvise (3)
impunity (5)
inarticulate (17)
incredible (20)
indefatigable (22)
indisposed (10)
indomitable (23)
inept (1)
infallible (8)
infirm (2)
inflict (15)
iniquitous (20)
initiative (17)
inlet (22)
inspire (6)
interminable (5)
intermittent (8)
intricate (18)
inured (11)

KINDLE (21)
knell (12)

LAMINATED (17)
legible (9)
lei (12)
livid (5)
locate (19)
loot (20)
lucid (18)
lurid (21)

MANSION (24)
maze (10)
melee (7)
memorable (9)
mentor (22)
mere (19)
merge (20)
mesa (15)
miniature (4)
minute (7)
mire (15)
misnomer (20)
mite (13)

Introduction

This book has four main purposes: (1) to help you learn new words, (2) to give you a better understanding of how words are formed and how they are used, (3) to give you some idea of where many of our words come from and some of the interesting stories behind them, and (4), perhaps most important from your point of view, to make the learning of this material interesting and enjoyable.

Here are a few tips to help you get the most out of the book:

Keep a dictionary close at hand as you do the exercises. You will need one that gives word origins. *Webster's New World Dictionary* in the Popular Library pocket-sized edition is recommended because it contains this information and is also quite inexpensive.

Make use of the Wordly Wise section which you will find at the end of most lessons. You may need to refer to this section while doing some of the exercises, so it is a good idea to read the section over thoroughly at the start of each lesson.

Remember that many words have more than one meaning. Don't be satisfied until you know *all* the meanings of a word and can use the word freely and comfortably. There are five exercises in each lesson; don't skip any of them.

The format of this book has been kept simple. The five exercises in each lesson are headed A, B, C, D, and E. All the A exercises are done in the same way; all the B exercises are done in the same way, and so on.

After each set of three lessons, there is a crossword puzzle which uses all the words you have learned in those three lessons. This review will help refresh your memory.

Certain terms are used in this book, and you should be thoroughly familiar with their meanings. These terms are as follows:

Synonym
A synonym is a word having the same or nearly the same meaning as another word in the same language. *Small* and *little* are synonyms, so are *talk* and *speak*.

Antonym
An antonym is a word having an opposite meaning to another word. *Up* and *down* are antonyms, so are *sad* and *happy*.

Homonym
A homonym is a word having the same pronunciation as another word but a different meaning and usually a different spelling. *Coarse* and *course* are homonyms, so are *bare* and *bear*.

Root
A root is a word or part of a word that is used as a base on which to make other words. The word *body* is a root since we can make such new words as *embody, disembodied, bodily* from it. *Ept* is a root, although it is not a word, because from it we can make such words as *adept* and *inept*.

Prefix
A prefix is a syllable or a group of syllables attached to the beginning of a word to change its meaning. Some common prefixes are *un-, non-, re-,* and *anti-*. Some others already mentioned in the above entry on roots are *em-, dis-, ad-,* and *in-*. Most of our prefixes have come to us from Greek or Latin.

Suffix
A suffix is a syllable or a group of syllables attached to the end of a word to change its meaning. Some common suffixes are *-ness, -ed, -er, -ly,* and *-able*. Many of our suffixes have come to us from Greek or Latin.

Let us put a root, suffix, and prefix together in an example. By adding the suffix -*ly* to the root *man*, we get the adjective *manly*, which means "brave" or "honorable." We can add a prefix *un* which means "not," and form a new adjective, *unmanly*, which means "cowardly" or "dishonorable."

If you come upon any of the above terms while working on the exercises in this book and are not sure of their meanings, turn back to the entries above.

Chapter One

Word List 1

ANTISEPTIC	EXEMPLARY	OFFAL
COHERENT	GRATITUDE	PLACID
DELIBERATE	INEPT	RETALIATE
DOLT	NEGLIGIBLE	RITE
ELAPSE	NYMPH	WILE

Look up the words above in your dictionary. Note that some of the words have more than one meaning. When you feel that you know *all* the meanings of *all* the words, go on to the exercise below.

EXERCISE 1A

From the four choices under each phrase or sentence, you are to mark the one that is closest in meaning to the word appearing in italics. When the same word appears more than once, you should note that it is being used in a different sense.

1. The punishment was *exemplary*.
   (a) completely undeserved (b) very mild (c) extremely severe (d) meant as a warning

2. *exemplary* conduct
   (a) worthy of being imitated (b) unreliable (c) becoming gradually worse (d) shameful

3. a feeling of *gratitude*
   (a) hope (b) extreme sorrow (c) helplessness (d) thankfulness

4. Who is that *dolt?*
   (a) very old man (b) small child (c) stupid person (d) inquisitive woman

5. Why don't they *retaliate?*
   (a) fight back (b) come back (c) return to work (d) complete the work

6. a *placid* lake
   (a) peaceful (b) very long and narrow (c) very deep (d) filled with fish

7. Where is the *antiseptic?*

   (a) remedy for poison (b) germ-killing substance (c) stain remover (d) soothing ointment

8. last *rites*
   (a) days of the year (b) religious acts (c) years of the century (d) theater performances

9. a *negligible* amount
   (a) huge (b) slight (c) unexpected (d) constantly changing

10. an *inept* performance
    (a) entertaining (b) clumsy (c) exciting (d) slow and stately

11. an *inept* remark
    (a) short and witty (b) cruel (c) foolishly incorrect (d) cleverly timed

12. a *coherent* whole
    (a) unchanging (b) connected (c) growing smaller (d) expanding

13. a *coherent* speech
    (a) very serious (b) rambling (c) amusing (d) clearly put together

14. a water *nymph*
    (a) nature goddess (b) carnival (c) flower shaped like a lily (d) fountain

15. a shepherd and his *nymph*
    (a) crooked stick (b) young helper (c) beautiful, young girl (d) group of sheep

16. One hour *elapsed*.
    (a) was sufficient (b) was needed (c) slipped by (d) remained

17. to *deliberate* for hours
    (a) wait anxiously (b) argue violently (c) discuss fully (d) sit quietly

18. a *deliberate* act
    (a) done in secrecy (b) careless (c) done on

1

purpose (d) meaningless

19. *deliberate* movements
(a) jerky (b) smooth (c) hurried (d) unhurried

20. using *wiles*
(a) acts of force (b) logical arguments (c) clever tricks (d) wooden supports

21. The *offal* can be thrown away.
(a) old and worn-out clothing (b) waste parts of slaughtered animals (c) dried out and hardened cement (d) food that has gone bad

Check your answers against the correct ones below. The answers are not in order; this is to prevent your eye catching sight of the correct ones before you have had a chance to do the exercise on your own.

6a. 12b. 17c. 4c. 8b. 1d. 9b. 3d. 11c. 14a. 10b. 20c. 16c. 19d. 13d. 18c. 7b. 2a. 21b. 15c. 5a.

Go back to your dictionary and look up again those words for which you gave incorrect answers. Only after doing this should you go on to the next exercise.

EXERCISE 1B

Each word from Word List 1 is used four times in the following sentences; one of the sentences in each group uses the word incorrectly. You are to circle the letter that precedes that sentence. Do not circle more than one letter in any group.

1. (a) How can we show our *gratitude* for all you have done for us? (b) The *gratitude* of the passengers rescued from the sinking ship knew no bounds. (c) The look of *gratitude* on her face was payment enough for my services. (d) It is very foolish of parents to *gratitude* every wish of their children.

2. (a) Try to set a good *exemplary* for the other children. (b) All my children had *exemplary* records at school. (c) The behavior of these soldiers was *exemplary* in every way. (d) A fine of ten thousand dollars may seem severe, but it is intended to be *exemplary*.

3. (a) If we are attacked, we will take *retaliatory* measures. (b) When will you *retaliate* the money that you borrowed? (c) The bombing of the cities is in *retaliation* for our attacks along the border yesterday. (d) Bill hits Jimmy, and when Jimmy *retaliates*, a fight breaks out.

4. (a) So much time has *elapsed* since she left that it seems useless to try to follow her now. (b) After talking without a pause for ten minutes, he suddenly *elapsed* into silence. (c) She sometimes lets months *elapse* before writing to her mother. (d) You must not open this letter until five years have *elapsed*.

5. (a) There are a few errors in the report, but they are quite *negligible*. (b) The police are trying to prove I was *negligible* in driving with faulty brakes. (c) I did lose some money, but it was a *negligible* amount. (d) There is a difference in the two sets of figures, but it is so *negligible* that it can be ignored.

6. (a) He handled the matter so *ineptly* that everyone's feelings were hurt. (b) She is such an *inept* dancer that she almost tripped over her own feet. (c) They put the shed together so *ineptly* that it collapsed after two days. (d) I find it hard to *inept* myself to these new methods.

7. (a) I'm afraid this cut will *antiseptic* unless we put something in it. (b) Joseph Lister, a nineteenth-century English doctor, is the father of modern *antiseptic* surgery. (c) Alcohol and iodine are both effective *antiseptics*. (d) The doctor's instruments must be washed in an *antiseptic* solution before they are used.

8. (a) He has lived his whole life in this *placid* little town, and he has no desire to move now. (b) Grandmother smiled *placidly* when I remarked on how well she was looking. (c) The lake is so *placid* today that I might try to swim

2

across it. (d) The *placid* was suddenly shattered by the sounds of heavy gunfire.

9. (a) *Nymphs* and shepherds come away; come and play the livelong day. (b) He planted rows of *nymphs* and marigolds along the border of his garden. (c) This is a picture of the goddess Aphrodite, surrounded by some of her *nymphs*. (d) The *nymphs* of field and woodland green, to human eyes remain unseen.

10. (a) You have *dolted* every chance you have ever had. (b) What a *dolt* I was to forget to ask his name. (c) Such *doltish* behavior is inexcusable. (d) Only a *dolt* like myself would have let her get away with it.

11. (a) Let the *coherent* dry for a few seconds before you press the broken edges together. (b) The four parts of the poem together form a *coherent* whole. (c) You have yet to write a *coherent* sentence for me. (d) He talked so *incoherently* that none of us understood a word of what he was saying.

12. (a) She took *deliberate* aim before squeezing the trigger. (b) The three judges *deliberated* for hours before reaching a verdict. (c) The prisoners were overjoyed at being *deliberated* from their prison. (d) You tripped her *deliberately*, didn't you?

13. (a) He used all his *wiles* to trap her into marrying him. (b) You have to watch him very carefully because he's such a *wily* fellow. (c) On a sudden *wile*, she took a plane to Los Angeles to see her mother. (d) Beware of the *wiles* of people who offer to make you rich overnight.

14. (a) The priest arrived just in time to give the last *rites* of the church to the dying man. (b) The service was conducted according to the *rites* of the church. (c) The marriage *rites* were performed in the little chapel by Rabbi Bernstein. (d) William the Conqueror claimed England by *rite* of conquest.

15. (a) The carcasses are cut up here, and the *offal* thrown away. (b) The *offal*, after being processed, is used as fertilizer. (c) The smell was so *offal* that we had to leave. (d) The livers, hearts, and *offal* are sold separately.

EXERCISE 1C

Rewrite each of the sentences below, replacing the italicized word or phrase with a word from Word List 1 and writing the word in the form that fits the rest of the sentence. Use each word only once. Write your answers in the spaces provided.

1. He made a *carefully thought-out* effort to gain our support by using flattery and other *sly tricks.*

.... coherent ....

.... wiles ....

2. You should put some *germ-killing substance* on that cut.

.... antiseptic ....

....

3. A statue of a *small nature goddess* stood on an island in the middle of the *calm and peaceful* lake.

.... nymph ....

.... placid ....

4. I feel like a *stupid person* when I am unable to put together a *clear, logically constructed* sentence.

.... dolt ....

.... coherent ....

5. They will not allow much time to *slip by* before they begin to *fight back.*

.... elapsed ....

.... *retaliate* ....

6. We throw the *waste parts of the slaughtered animals* into these barrels while the rest of the carcass is cut up and frozen.

.... *offal* ....

....

7. The way you acted was *a model of good behavior,* and I would like to express my *very deep thanks* for what you did.

.... *exemplary* ....

.... *gratitude* ....

8. Some of the *religious ceremonies* of the Eastern churches seem very strange to us.

.... *rites* ....

....

9. Fortunately, the damage caused by his *awkward, clumsy* handling of the situation is *very slight and can be ignored*.

.... *inept* ....

.... *negligible* ....

EXERCISE 1D

The following questions deal with prefixes and roots. If you are not sure what is meant by these terms, you should turn back to the Introduction, where you will find them fully explained.

ANTISEPTIC is made up of the Greek root *septic,* meaning "causing infection," and the Greek prefix *anti-,* meaning "against." Thus, an antiseptic is a substance that works *against infection.*

Look over the following words. If necessary, check them in a dictionary that gives word origins. In only three of them is *anti-* used as a prefix meaning "against"; you are to circle the two words that are *NOT* made up of *anti-* plus a root.

antic   antidote   antislavery   antique   antibiotic

Three of the following words can be used as roots to make new words with the addition of the prefix *anti-.* Circle the two words that *cannot* be used in this way.

knock   cyclone   quaint   body   quarry

1. *Sympathy* means having strong feelings *for* someone or something; .... means having strong feelings *against* someone.

2. A gun used to fire against aircraft would be called an .... gun.

3. *Macassar* is the name of a hair oil once used by men. To keep it from getting on the backs of chairs where men rested their heads, a special cloth was placed over the chair back. Such a cloth would be called an ....

EXERCISE 1E

Write out, in the spaces provided, the words from Word List 1 for which a definition, homonym, synonym, or antonym is given on the next page. (Explanations of these terms are given in the Introduction.) When you are asked to give a root or a prefix, you should refer back to the preceding exercise; the information you require will be found there. Make sure that each of your answers has the same number of letters as there are spaces.

If all the words are filled in correctly, the boxes running up and down the answer spaces will give you the first six words of a quotation from Sir Winston Churchill, a man who has been described as "the greatest Englishman of our times." The quotation is from his book **My Early Life** and will be continued in Exercise 2E.

1. a homonym for *right*

r i t e

2. a trick

3. to do harm in return for harm

4. a substance that kills germs

w i l e
r e t a l i a t e
a n t i s e p t i c

5. an antonym for *rambling*

6. Greek prefix meaning "against"

7. a synonym for *commendable*

8. an antonym for *skillful*

9. a nature goddess

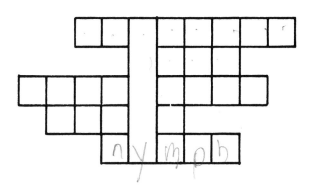

n y m p h

10. the waste parts of a slaughtered animal

11. to slip by or pass by (said of time)

o f f a l
e l a p s e

12. a feeling of being thankful

G r a t i t u d e

13. an antonym for *excited*

14. an antonym for *hasty*

15. a synonym for *slight*

16. a synonym for *simpleton*

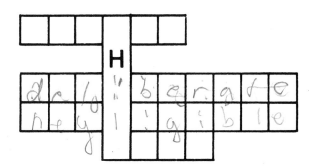

H

d e l i b e r a t e
n e g l i g i b l e

The same word may sometimes be pronounced differently to indicate its part of speech. Check DELIBERATE in your dictionary and note that it is pronounced one way when it is a verb and another way when it is an adjective.

EXEMPLARY is spelled with an *e* while *example* has an *a* for its third letter. These two words share a similarity of meaning; if you set a good *example* to others, your behavior could fairly be called *exemplary*.

Alchemists were the forerunners of today's scientists. Their aim was not to discover scientific truths but to change base metals such as lead into precious metals such as gold. Those who claimed (falsely, of course) to be able to do this called themselves *adeptus* from the Latin word for *attained;* they had "attained" the alchemists' goal. Later, shortened to *adept*, the word came to mean *skillful* as in the sentence "He is *adept* at all field sports." When it was found necessary to form the opposite of this word, it was done by changing the prefix from *ad-*, meaning "nearness to," to *in-*, meaning "lacking; without." Thus, the word INEPT was formed.

Don't confuse NEGLIGIBLE, which means "slight," with *negligent,* which means "failing to do what is required; careless."

When the carcass of a slaughtered animal is being trimmed by a butcher, certain waste parts are cut away and allowed to fall. OFFAL, our word for such waste parts, comes to us from Middle English (the language spoken in England from around A.D. 1100 to 1500) and simply means the parts that fall off, or *off fall*.

Note carefully these different spellings: *right, write*, and RITE. These three words are homonyms. Some people pronounce the next two words as though they were homonyms; they are not. WILE is pronounced as it is spelled; *while* is pronounced with the breath around the *w* —*hwile*.

Word List 2

AGITATE	EMBEZZLE	NUTRIENT
APPREHENSIVE	EQUINE	OPPORTUNE
ASSET	FERRET	PASTORAL
CAMOUFLAGE	GLOWER	RHETORIC
CANTER	INFIRM	WREST

Look up the words above in your dictionary. Note that some of the words have more than one meaning. When you feel that you know *all* the meanings of *all* the words, go on to the following exercise.

EXERCISE 2A

From the four choices under each phrase or sentence, you are to mark the one that is closest in meaning to the word appearing in italics. When the same word appears more than once, you should note that it is being used in a different sense.

1. We must *camouflage* the guns.
   (a) prepare to abandon (b) prepare to fire (c) put out of action (d) disguise in order to hide

2. the company's *assets*
   (a) debts (b) shareholders (c) property (d) records

3. a useful *asset*
   (a) pause in fighting (b) thing of value (c) remark (d) suggestion

4. *pastoral* poetry
   (a) difficult to understand (b) unrhymed and with lines of uneven length (c) written for children (d) suggestive of country life

5. *pastoral* duties
   (a) weekly (b) priestly (c) carefully outlined (d) irregular

6. He uses a *ferret* to hunt rabbits.
   (a) gun with two barrels (b) short bow powered with a spring (c) short, heavy club (d) small animal like a weasel

7. to *ferret out* the true story
   (a) cover up (b) be unwilling to believe (c) search out (d) understand

8. The conditions were *opportune*.
   (a) getting better (b) just right for the purpose (c) getting worse (d) not suitable for what was planned

9. She seems very *apprehensive.*
   (a) easily angered (b) fearful of what might happen (c) overjoyed by her good fortune (d) willing to do what she is told.

10. *equine* diseases
    (a) of horses (b) of cows (c) of pigs (d) of sheep

11. to *glower* at someone
    (a) shout (b) stare angrily (c) smile pleasantly (d) strike back

12. attempting to *embezzle*
    (a) recover stolen money (b) escape while being held captive (c) steal money by the use of threats (d) steal money placed in one's care

13. He rode at a *canter.*
    (a) fast walking pace (b) slow gallop (c) English stable (d) private club

14. to *wrest* control
    (a) give up unwillingly (b) give up willingly (c) obtain after a struggle (d) obtain without effort

15. What *nutrients* are in this?
    (a) kinds of metals (b) harmful substances (c) unknown substances (d) substances having food value

16. the art of *rhetoric*
    (a) trapping wild animals (b) the skillful use of color (c) the skillful use of words (d) warfare using modern weapons

17. No *rhetoric* please!
    (a) arguments (b) playful joking (c) showy language (d) bad language

18. an *infirm* old man
    (a) fit (b) weak (c) cheerful (d) gloomy

19. This *agitates* the mixture.
    (a) spreads (b) shakes up (c) separates (d) hardens

20. She seems very *agitated.*
    (a) shy (b) lovely (c) tired (d) disturbed

21. to *agitate* for better conditions
    (a) show unconcern (b) take credit (c) arouse support (d) wait patiently

Check your answers against the correct ones below. The answers are not in order; this is to prevent your eye catching sight of the correct ones before you have had a chance to do the exercise on your own.

7c. 12d. 9b. 4d. 20d. 15d. 2c. 10a. 1d. 16c. 11b. 14c. 6d. 18b. 5b. 17c. 13b. 8b. 19b. 3b. 21c.

Go back to your dictionary and look up again those words for which you gave incorrect answers. Only after doing this should you go on to the next exercise.

EXERCISE 2B

Each word from Word List 2 is used four times in the sentences below; one of the sentences in each group uses the word incorrectly. You are to circle the letter that precedes that sentence. Do not circle more than one letter in any one group.

1. (a) Her remarks were most *opportune* and helped to smooth over the difficulties we had been having. (b) Your arrival at the meeting was most *opportune.* (c) I hope you will give me an *opportune* to show what I can do. (d) I've been waiting for an *opportune* moment to mention the matter to him.

2. (a) The *assets* of the company include its land, buildings, machinery, cash, and money owed to it. (b) Her clear thinking and continual energy are her greatest *assets.* (c) The company's *assets* exceed five million dollars. (d) I would *asset* the damage to the barn at about five hundred dollars.

3. (a) The parcel looked *apprehensive* so we called in the police to open it. (b) A feeling of *apprehension* gripped her when she heard footsteps coming from one of the bedrooms. (c) She became *apprehensive* when we asked

7

her if she had seen her son lately. (d) She looked nervously at me, *apprehensive* of what I would say.

4. (a) After a short vacation, the priest was delighted to return to his *pastoral* duties. (b) She did the portrait in blue, yellow, and pink *pastorals*. (c) This painter is noted chiefly for his *pastoral* landscapes. (d) Christopher Marlowe's poem "The Passionate Shepherd to His Love" is a fine example of *pastoral* poetry.

5. (a) You should get rid of a horse as soon as it starts to *equine*. (b) She is an expert on *equine* diseases. (c) It is hard to believe that the huge Clydesdale, weighing nearly a ton, and the tiny Shetland pony are both *equines*. (d) Of all the members of the *equine* family, the full-blooded Arabian is the noblest.

6. (a) I received my prize with a smile, ignoring the *glowers* of the boys I had beaten. (b) Don't *glower* at me when I'm speaking to you! (c) They *glowered* at me when I took their ball, but they were afraid to try to get it back. (d) She *glowered* her eyebrows in a grim scowl.

7. (a) If you have served time in prison as an *embezzler,* you are unlikely to gain a responsible job in a bank. (b) Thieves broke into the house last night and *embezzled* two fur coats and some jewelry. (c) When the accountants balance the company's books, they will discover the *embezzlement.* (d) The police believe he *embezzled* nearly fifty thousand dollars over the ten years he worked for the company.

8. (a) She threw a *canter* over the horse and led it out of the stable. (b) Don't take the horse faster than a *canter.* (c) The riders *cantered* around the ring. (d) The horses *cantered* across the field toward me, knowing that I was going to feed them.

9. (a) After a sharp struggle he *wrested* the gun from the robber's hand. (b) Rebel troops *wrested* control of the government from the king in yesterday's fighting. (c) She *wrested* with the problem for hours before finally solving it. (d) The peasants work very hard to *wrest* a living from the barren soil.

10. (a) The blood carries *nutrients* to build up all the cells in your body. (b) This pet food contains all the *nutrients* your cat needs. (c) She's such a fussy eater that she won't touch *nutrients*. (d) Has this food been tested for its *nutrient* properties?

11. (a) Those who are too *infirm* to walk will be allowed to ride. (b) She was a very old woman, bowed down by the *infirmities* of her age. (c) Those who are needed will be *infirmed* by mail. (d) We must set up an *infirmary* to look after the wounded.

12. (a) "Are you men or are you mice?" he asked *rhetorically*. (b) There was much *rhetoric* but little substance in his speech. (c) Anyone going into politics would do well to study the art of *rhetoric*. (d) He grinned *rhetorically* at the cheering crowd.

13. (a) The sudden gusts of wind *agitated* the surface of the lake. (b) He became very *agitated* when I said he could not see the mayor without an appointment. (c) The pole vaulter *agitated* himself gracefully over the bar. (d) For many years she *agitated* for a lowering of the voting age to eighteen.

14. (a) We *camouflaged* the money by burying it in the garden. (b) We *camouflaged* ourselves with leafy branches torn from the trees. (c) This shoeshine parlor was just a *camouflage* for gambling activities. (d) The tiger's stripes are an effective *camouflage* against the jungle greenery.

15. (a) He *ferreted* his money away in hiding places all over his house. (b) I was determined to *ferret* out the truth. (c) After the rabbits have been *ferreted* out of their holes, they are trapped in these nets. (d) The *ferret*

has a long body like a weasel, little red eyes, and very sharp teeth!

EXERCISE 2C

Rewrite each of the sentences below, replacing the italicized word or phrase with a word from Word List 2 and writing the word in the form that fits the rest of the sentence. Use each word only once. Write your answers in the spaces provided.

1. If I ride my horse faster than a *slow and easy gallop,* I become somewhat *uneasy about what may happen.*

   .... *canter* ....

   .... *apprehensive* ....

2. The *weak and feeble* condition of the prisoners is due to the lack of proper *nourishing substances* in their food.

   .... *infirm* ....

   .... *nutrients* ....

3. By making skillful use of every *thing of value that he owned,* he was able to *win, after a short struggle,* complete control of the company from his former bosses.

   .... *asset* ....

   .... *wrest* ....

4. She did *steal money that was entrusted to her,* almost $5000, and she can do nothing to *cover up* the fact.

   .... *embezzle* ....

   .... *camouflage* ....

5. When we felt the time was *right for our purpose,* we began to *try to arouse interest in and support* for a new children's playground.

   .... *opportune* ....

.... *agitate* ....

6. He *looked angrily* at me when I remarked that he had somewhat *horse-like* features.

   .... *glowered* ....

   .... *equine* ....

7. This is a long poem, chiefly dealing with *life in the country and other peaceful* subjects, and only occasionally marred by the poet's flashy use of *exaggerated language.*

   .... *pastoral* ....

   .... *rhetoric* ....

8. After *making a thorough search* all through the house, the police were unable to discover a single clue.

   .... *ferreting* ....

   ....

EXERCISE 2D

The following questions deal with roots, prefixes, and suffixes. If you are not sure what is meant by these terms, you should turn back to the Introduction, where you will find them fully explained.

The same root is often found in a number of words, and usually these words will be related in meaning. In APPREHENSIVE, the root is *prehend* (also written *prehens*) from the Latin word meaning "to grasp; to seize." When you are "seized" with fear, you are *apprehensive.*

Using the root *prehend* or *prehens,* complete the words below for which prefixes and suffixes have been supplied. Write out a brief definition of each word, checking in your dictionary for accuracy of spelling and meaning.

1. C O M _____

....

2. A P _____

. . . .

3. R E _____

. . . .

4. C O M _____ I V E

. . . .

APPREHENSIVE is made from the Latin root *prehens*, meaning "seize," together with the prefix *ad-*, meaning "to; toward," and the suffix *-ive*, meaning "having the nature of; given to." In your own words, explain why you think the prefix *ad-* became changed to *ap-*.

. . . .

. . . .

Circle the name of the animal that has a *prehensile* tail:

elephant   monkey   tiger   rabbit

By adding or taking away prefixes or suffixes, we change the meanings of words.

1. By adding a suffix to INFIRM, we get a word meaning "a place for sick people." What is this word?

. . . .

2. By removing the suffix from PASTORAL, we get a word meaning "a clergyman or priest." What is this word?

. . . .

3. By adding a suffix to OPPORTUNE, we get a word meaning "a person who takes advantage of opportunities regardless of harm done to others." What is this word?

. . . .

EXERCISE 2E

Write out, in the spaces provided, the words from Word List 2 for which a definition, homonym, synonym, or antonym is given on the next page. When you are asked to give a root or a prefix, you should refer back to the preceding exercise; the information you require will be found there. Make sure that each of your answers has the same number of letters as there are spaces. A definition followed by a number is a review word; the number gives the Word List from which it is taken.

If all the words are filled in correctly, the boxes running up and down the answer spaces will continue the quotation begun earlier.

1. to stare angrily

2. of or like a horse

3. to stir up; excite

4. the skillful use of words in speaking or writing

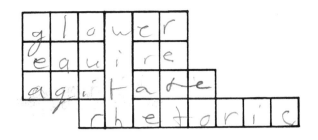

5. to steal money placed in one's care

6. a nature goddess (1)

7. an antonym for *untimely*

8. a stupid person (1)

9. having to do with priests and their duties

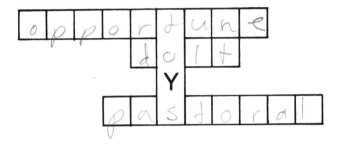

10. a suffix meaning "having the nature of"

11. a slow gallop

12. a substance having food value

13. a synonym for *fearful*

14. to search out

15. awkward; clumsy (1)

16. to disguise in order to hide

17. an antonym for *healthy*

18. anything owned that has value

19. a Latin root meaning "seize"

20. a synonym for *seize*

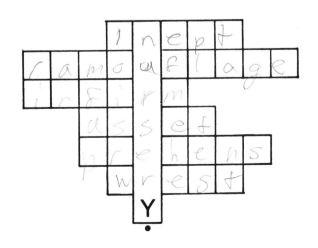

WORDLY WISE 2

CAMOUFLAGE is a word to be wary of. It comes to us from France and retains both its French spelling and pronunciation.

Think back for a moment to two thousand years ago. How would you feel if you were a Roman sailor who had been at sea for many weeks? When your ship finally entered port, would you not regard that as an *opportune* moment to start doing all the things you had planned while at sea? A Roman sailor would probably feel this way. Our word OPPORTUNE comes from the Latin *ob,* meaning "before," and *portus,* meaning "port." Incidentally, the Roman god who protected ports and harbors was *Portunus;* August 7th was a feast day in his honor.

Let us follow the path of the Latin root *past* (also written *pasc*) through our language. The word originally meant "to graze; to feed on grass," and we can see from this definition how our word *pasture* is derived. The Latin word *pastor,* meaning

"shepherd," comes from this root and was taken into English with the same meaning. Priests from the earliest days of Christianity have been looked upon as shepherds to their faithful bands of worshippers; such men also came to be known as *pastors.* PASTORAL duties are priestly duties; however, this adjective still retains its original meaning "having to do with shepherds" now broadened to mean "having to do with the countryside, particularly in its more peaceful aspects." A *pastoral* is a poem dealing with the peaceful life of the countryside; a *pastorale* (with a final "e") is a piece of music that suggests to the listeners the same sort of subject.

RHETORIC is pronounced with the stress on the first syllable; *rhetorical* shifts the stress onto the second syllable. A "rhetorical question" is one asked by a speaker purely for effect; no answer is required or expected.

Word List 3

AFFRONT	FLOE	RADIANT
CONFER	HABITUAL	RECEDE
EERIE	IMPROVISE	SLOVENLY
EXTRAORDINARY	PALLID	SOCIABLE
FERVOR	PERPETUAL	WREATHE

Look up the words above in your dictionary. Note that some of the words have more than one meaning. When you feel that you know *all* the meanings of *all* the words, go on to the following exercise.

EXERCISE 3A

From the four choices under each phrase or sentence, you are to mark the one that is closest in meaning to the word appearing in italics. When the same word appears more than once, you should note that it is being used in a different sense.

1. *slovenly* habits
   (a) fixed (b) neat (c) expensive (d) messy

2. She ignored the *affront.*
   (a) greeting (b) insult (c) piece of bad news (d) threat

3. *eerie* sounds

(a) pleasant (b) mysterious (c) piercing (d) muffled

4. Try to be more *sociable.*
   (a) accurate at adding figures (b) reserved in dealing with people (c) active in sports and athletics (d) friendly in the company of others

5. to *confer* with the governor
   (a) dine (b) travel (c) disagree (d) talk

6. to *confer* a title
   (a) grant (b) receive (c) give up (d) seek

7. a *perpetual* noise
   (a) very loud (b) strange (c) very soft (d) constant

8. *perpetual* fame
   (a) well-deserved (b) uncertain (c) brief (d) lasting forever

9. a *radiant* smile
   (a) crooked (b) forced (c) beaming (d) sly

10. *radiant* heat
    (a) that keeps stopping and starting (b) that is

given off in rays (c) that is produced at low cost (d) that is conducted through a substance

11. Look out for *floes!*
    (a) fish that travel with the current (b) logs that float underwater (c) small sailboats (d) large floating sheets of ice

12. to *wreathe* flowers
    (a) twist into a ring (b) sell on street corners (c) grow in window boxes (d) transplant to better soil

13. filled with *fervor*
    (a) sudden fear (b) intense emotion (c) deep respect (d) anxiety

14. an *habitual* act
    (a) often repeated (b) unexpected (c) amusing (d) cruel

15. his *habitual* chair
    (a) leather-covered (b) comfortable (c) worn-out (d) usual

16. Her face was *pallid*.
    (a) long and thin (b) without color (c) healthy looking (d) round and chubby

17. The floodwaters began to *recede*.
    (a) drop back (b) wash away the soil (c) overflow the riverbanks (d) get higher and higher

18. a *receding* chin
    (a) square (b) pointed (c) sticking out (d) sloping back

19. an *extraordinary* victory
    (a) well-deserved (b) remarkable (c) eagerly awaited (d) temporary

20. What *extraordinary* clothes!
    (a) expensive (b) soft and clinging (c) very sensible (d) very unusual

21. She *improvised* on the piano.
    (a) played badly (b) displayed good technique (c) made up melodies on the spur of the moment (d) played along with another person

Check your answers against the correct ones below. The answers are not in order; this is to prevent your eye catching sight of the correct ones before you have had a chance to do the exercise on your own.

9c. 4d. 13b. 11d. 7d. 20d. 15d. 6a. 1d. 16b. 5d. 12a. 18d. 10b. 3b. 14a. 8d. 2b. 17a. 19b. 21c.

Go back to your dictionary and look up again those words for which you gave incorrect answers. Only after doing this should you go on to the next exercise.

EXERCISE 3B

Each word from Word List 3 is used four times in the sentences below; one of the sentences in each group uses the word incorrectly. You are to circle the letter that precedes that sentence. Do not circle more than one letter in any one group.

1. (a) The light from my torch cast *eerie* shadows on the wall. (b) The *eerie* sounds of the forest kept us awake for hours on the first night of our camping trip. (c) The eagle returned to its *eerie*, carrying in its claws a rabbit it had killed. (d) The *eeriest* creature of the ocean depths is the giant squid.

2. (a) He had the *pallid* complexion of a man who stays indoors most of the time. (b) The walls and ceilings were painted a *pallid* green. (c) She seemed at first to be an interesting person, but the pleasure of her company began to *pallid* after a few days. (d) The *pallid* cheeks and weak voice of the old man told me that he was very near death.

3. (a) Our new neighbors seem very *sociable*. (b) If you want to make friends, you will have to be more *sociable* with people. (c) Because ants and bees live in highly-organized groups or colonies, they are called *sociable* insects. (d) It was not very *sociable* of her to leave the party just when everyone was beginning to have a good time.

4. (a) I will not easily forgive such a deliberate *affront*. (b) He quickly confessed when *affronted* with the evidence of his crime.

13

(c) I'm afraid you *affronted* him by yawning while he was talking. (d) When none of us touched the food she had prepared, the cook took it as a personal *affront*.

5. (a) She dresses so *slovenly* that I am ashamed to be seen with her. (b) She may be a *slovenly* dresser but that is because she has never been taught how to wear clothes properly. (c) The work was done in such a *slovenly* manner that I made him do the whole thing over. (d) He *slovenlied* about the house in a dirty bathrobe.

6. (a) I have listened very carefully to you, and I *confer* with everything you had to say. (b) The university will *confer* the degree of Doctor of Laws on her in tomorrow's ceremony. (c) The president *conferred* for over an hour yesterday with his military advisers. (d) Many distinguished scientists will be speaking at the *conference*.

7. (a) The winner's face was *wreathed* in smiles as she accepted the first prize. (b) Would you help me *wreathe* these flowers around the wire frames? (c) Every year the old woman places a small *wreathe* on her husband's grave. (d) Grandfather sat back in his armchair contentedly watching the blue smoke *wreathe* from his pipe.

8. (a) The calypso singers of the Caribbean islands often *improvise* verses while they are singing. (b) She was able to play the *improvise* all the way through just from memory. (c) We *improvised* a sail out of an old bedsheet. (d) There aren't enough chairs and tables, so we will just have to *improvise*.

9. (a) We can make this cabin *habitual* by filling in the cracks in the walls and repairing the doors and windows. (b) "Are you an *habitual* smoker?" the doctor asked. (c) Uncle Ben *habitually* wore a red carnation in his buttonhole. (d) When Father and Mother went to their *habitual* places in the church, they found two strangers sitting in them.

10. (a) With the score tied and less than five minutes left to go, the *fervor* of the crowd knew no bounds. (b) Despite the speaker's attempts to arouse them, the crowds were noticeably lacking in *fervor*. (c) A sudden power failure at the prison *fervored* the escape of the two prisoners. (d) She spoke so *fervently* that all who heard her were convinced.

11. (a) Consider for a moment the unceasing ebb and *floe* of the tides. (b) The ice *floes* drift with the current until they melt in the warmer waters to the south. (c) The huge *floes*, formed when the ice fields break up in the spring, are a danger to shipping in the area. (d) From the ship we would sometimes see walrus sunning themselves while perched on an ice *floe*.

12. (a) The danger of enemy attack has *receded* sufficiently for us to allow people to go freely about their business. (b) They *receded* that they had been beaten fairly and squarely. (c) He has a rather long face with close-set eyes and a *receding* chin. (d) As the tide *recedes*, you can see hundreds of little crabs scurrying about on the rocks.

13. (a) I'll always remember how *radiant* she looked on her wedding day. (b) At night the monument was bathed in a *radiant* light. (c) The *radiant* heat of the sun is the source of all life here on earth. (d) All the streets of the town *radiant* out from a central point.

14. (a) He wore a *perpetual* frown on his face, as though he were deeply worried about something. (b) My new job keeps me *perpetually* on the move. (c) Amelia Earhart won *perpetual* fame by being the first woman to fly alone across the Atlantic. (d) Carnegie Hall was so named to *perpetual* the name of Andrew Carnegie.

15. (a) I like wearing clothes that are a little out of the *extraordinary*. (b) He told an *extraordinary*

story of how he was taken aboard a flying saucer. (c) His ability to memorize what he reads is *extraordinary*. (d) She is *extraordinarily* beautiful.

EXERCISE 3C

Rewrite each of the sentences below, replacing the italicized word or phrase with a word from Word List 3 and writing the word in the form that fits the rest of the sentence. Use each word only once. Write your answers in the spaces provided.

1. He said it would be an *insult* to his dignity to *meet for a discussion* with anyone but the governor.

   .... *affront* ....

   .... *confer* ....

2. Flowers were *twisted in circles* around the wooden columns on the porch.

   .... *wreathed* ....

   ....

3. He seems very *friendly in the company of others,* but what a pity he is such a *careless and untidy* dresser.

   .... *sociable* ....

   .... *slovenly* ....

4. It is *remarkable* how well he is able to *make up on the spur of the moment* such lovely tunes.

   .... *extraordinary* ....

   .... *improvise* ....

5. The villagers cannot return to their homes until the flood waters have begun to *drop back*.

   .... *recede* ....

6. The *strange and mysterious* silence was broken only by the large *sheets of floating ice* striking against the sides of the vessel.

   .... *eerie* ....

   .... *floes* ....

7. The speaker's face was *an unhealthy pale color*, but her eyes shone with an *intense passion* that was a little frightening.

   .... *pallid* ....

   .... *fervor* ....

8. Dressed in her *usual* flowered dress, the old woman who ran the fruit stall had a *beaming* smile for all her customers.

   .... *habitual* ....

   .... *radiant* ....

9. To those who live near an airport, the *constant* noise of jets taking off and landing is a great annoyance.

   .... *perpetual* ....

   ....

EXERCISE 3D

The word SOCIABLE is made up of the Latin root *socius,* meaning "companion," and the suffix *-able,* meaning "having qualities of." A sociable person is one having the qualities of a companion. Using this root, complete the words below for which the prefixes and suffixes have been supplied. Write out a brief definition of each word.

1. A N T I _____

   ....

2. _____ L O G Y

   ....

3. _____ T Y

. . . .

4. U N _____ A B L E

. . . .

5. _____ L I T E

. . . .

Circle each word below that does not end with the suffix -able.

usable   unstable   passable   laughable   cable

A very common Latin or French prefix is re-, meaning "back." Thus, RECEDE means "to move back." Write out, in the spaces provided, the five words defined below, all of which begin with the prefix re-. Select your answers from the following words: rebate, repress, recover, recoil, recall.

1. to draw *back,* as in fear

. . . .

2. money that is given *back*

. . . .

3. to call *back,* or bring *back,* to mind

. . . .

4. to get *back* something that was lost

. . . .

5. to hold *back,* as a sigh or tears

. . . .

Circle each word below that does not begin with the prefix re-.

reaper   respond   retract   reason   reckon

Write out *three* words from your dictionary that begin with the prefix re- and end with the suffix -able.

. . . .

. . . .

. . . .

EXERCISE 3E

Write out, in the spaces provided, the words from Word List 3 for which a definition, homonym, synonym, or antonym is given on the next page. When you are asked to give a root or a prefix, you should refer back to the preceding exercise; the information you require will be found there. Make sure that each of your answers has the same number of letters as there are spaces. A definition followed by a number is a review word; the number gives the Word List from which it is taken.

If all the words are filled in correctly, the boxes running up and down the answer spaces will continue the quotation begun earlier.

1. lacking color; pale

`p a l l i d`

2. skillful use of words (2)

3. shining brightly; beaming

4. an antonym for *indifference*

5. a homonym for *flow*

```
        r h e t o r i c
          r a d i a n t
    f e r v o r
    f l o e
```

6. an antonym for *unfriendly*

7. something owned that has value (2)

8. an antonym for *advance*

9. a synonym for *insult*

```
  s o c i a b l e
    a s s e t
    r e c e d e
a f f r o n t
```

10. logically connected (1)

11. a Latin suffix meaning "having qualities of"

12. lasting forever

13. to make do with what one has

14. fixed; usual

15. to meet for a talk or discussion

16. to twist or wind around

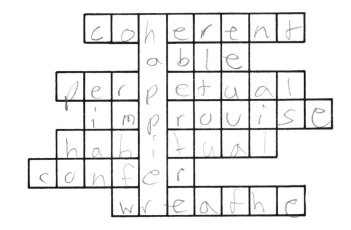

```
  c o h e r e n t
      a b l e
  p e r p e t u a l
    i m p r o v i s e
    h a b i t u a l
  c o n f e r
      w r e a t h e
```

17. a synonym for *weird*

18. an antonym for *neat*

19. a prefix meaning "back"

20. most unusual; remarkable

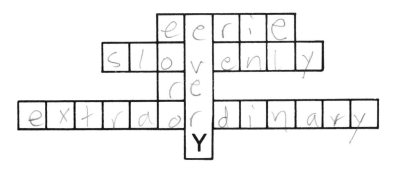

```
      e e r i e
    s l o v e n l y
      r e
e x t r a o r d i n a r y
      Y
```

17

EERIE means "mysterious; weird" and may be spelled *eery;* an eagle's nesting place is called an *aerie,* also spelled *aery.* Try not to confuse these two words and remember that the "ie" ending for both words is the preferred one.

When Noah Webster (1758-1843) wrote the first American dictionary, he simplified the spelling of many words. One of the changes he made was in words ending in the British spelling of *-our,* which we now end in *-or.* The English still use the *our* spelling; hence they write *fervour* while in this country we write FERVOR.

A person improvising on the piano is *not* able to *see* what the results will be *before* he has played the notes. If we write out in Latin the italicized words, we get *im* (not) + *pro* (before) + *vis* (see); from these three words we get our word IMPROVISE.

WREATHE is a verb meaning "to coil or twist around in circles." The *th* is pronounced as it is in *then.* Don't confuse this word with *wreath,* which is a noun meaning "a ring of twisted flowers or leaves." The *th* in this word is pronounced like the *th* in *thin.*

Social and SOCIABLE are similar in meaning but *social* has a broader definition applying both to animals and human beings, "living together in groups" (ants are *social* insects), while *sociable* refers only to people and means "taking pleasure from the company of others."

You have now studied and worked with a total of forty-five words in this first chapter. The next exercise will give you a chance to use all of these words. The crossword puzzle on the following page has forty-five clues; each clue is a definition of a word you have studied. Each word from Word Lists 1, 2, and 3 is used once, and always in the form in which it appears in the Word List.

Each chapter in this book will end with a crossword puzzle, and each puzzle will use all the words from the three Word Lists in that chapter plus a number of review words from earlier chapters. You can spot the review words easily because their clues are followed by a number which gives the Word List from which they are taken.

ACROSS

1. of or like a horse
4. suitable; timely
8. to have a talk
9. an insult
10. to disguise in order to hide
13. fearful; uneasy
15. anything owned that has value
16. beaming; bright
17. worthy of imitation
19. a stupid person
22. nourishing
24. endless; continuing
27. to make up quickly
29. to return harm for harm
31. a trick
32. skillful use of language
33. to stir up; to excite
34. awkward; clumsy
35. a slow gallop
37. to think over carefully
38. done by habit; fixed
39. careless; messy
40. to steal money in one's care

DOWN

1. remarkable; very unusual
2. weak; feeble
3. free from germs
5. calm; peaceful
6. to pass, as time
7. to get after a struggle
8. logically connected
11. the waste parts of slaughtered animals
12. to search out
14. pale
18. a religious act or ceremony
20. great strength of feeling
21. an angry stare
22. unimportant; trifling
23. a nature goddess
25. a feeling of being grateful
26. of the country; rural
28. friendly; talkative
30. weird; strange
31. to twist or wind around
32. to draw back
36. a large sheet of floating ice

Chapter Two

Word List 4

ABYSS	NAIVE	STIGMATIZE
BILLOW	RECOUP	SUPPLE
DEPRIVE	RICKETY	TUMBREL
EXCEL	SCRUPLE	WELT
IMMERSE	STAPLE	WRITHE
MINIATURE		

Look up the words above in your dictionary. Note that some of the words have more than one meaning. When you feel that you know *all* the meanings of *all* the words, go on to the exercise below.

EXERCISE 4A

From the four choices under each phrase or sentence, you are to mark the one that is closest in meaning to the word appearing in italics. When the same word appears more than once, you should note that it is being used in a different sense.

1. a *staple* of the country
   (a) important river (b) chief product (c) major city (d) famous landmark

2. We need *staples*.
   (a) cleaning materials (b) floor coverings (c) sugar, flour, etc. (d) writing paper, envelopes

3. a box of *staples*
   (a) flat-headed nails (b) rounded screws (c) colored pins (d) wire fasteners

4. to *deprive* them of it
   (a) keep from having (b) keep reminding (c) tell (d) keep from knowing

5. the edge of the *abyss*
   (a) shallow lake (b) frozen sea (c) deep opening (d) dense jungle

6. *abysmal* ignorance
   (a) immeasurably great (b) pretended (c) widespread (d) inexcusable

7. *supple* branches
   (a) leafy (b) fragile (c) sturdy (d) bending easily

8. a *supple* mind
   (a) adaptable (b) idle (c) deceitful (d) trained

9. They will *stigmatize* him.
   (a) do everything to help (b) give a bad name to (c) make good the damage done to (d) have nothing to do with

10. to *immerse* the plates
    (a) decorate the edges of (b) warm slightly (c) put into water (d) repair cracks in

11. to *excel* in sports
    (a) do better than others (b) show an interest (c) do poorly (d) have no interest

12. *miniature* figures
    (a) highly decorated (b) very small (c) hand carved (d) carefully drawn

13. a *miniature* of a woman
    (a) small statue (b) full length portrait (c) plaster figure (d) small picture

14. He didn't *scruple* to take the money.
    (a) have any reason (b) feel it wrong (c) tell anyone (d) fail

15. a painful *welt*
    (a) bullet wound (b) mark caused by a blow (c) pulled muscle (d) broken bone

16. the *welt* of a shoe
    (a) decorative holes punched in the top. (b) raised piece that supports the arch (c) strap that ties around the ankle (d) strip joining the upper to the sole

17. The *tumbrel* moved past.
    (a) cart (b) hay wagon (c) sled (d) trolley

18. to *recoup* one's losses
(a) estimate (b) get back (c) regret (d) not care about

19. She seems very *naive.*
(a) casual (b) timid (c) confident (d) inexperienced

20. *rickety* stairs
(a) winding (b) shaky (c) wooden (d) unpainted

21. The *billow* rocked the boat.
(a) wind (b) large wave (c) current (d) storm

22. The sail *billowed* in the wind.
(a) swelled out (b) collapsed (c) moved slightly (d) fluttered

23. to *writhe* in agony
(a) cry out (b) be (c) cause another person to be (d) twist and turn

24. to *writhe* inwardly
(a) want revenge (b) suffer shame (c) be content (d) be radiantly happy

Check your answers against the correct ones below. The answers are not in order; this is to prevent your eye catching sight of the correct ones before you have had a chance to do the exercise on your own.

9b. 3d. 14b. 7d. 17a. 8a. 21b. 15b. 11a. 1b. 20b. 22a. 6a. 5c. 19d. 18b. 23d. 4a. 16d. 2c. 10c. 12b. 13d. 24b.

Go back to your dictionary and look up again those words for which you gave incorrect answers. Only after doing this should you go on to the next exercise.

EXERCISE 4B

Each word from Word List 4 is used four times in the following sentences; one of the sentences in each group uses the word incorrectly. You are to circle the letter that precedes that sentence. Do not circle more than one letter in any one group.

1. (a) The *welt* on my shoe needs stitching. (b) He put on a pair of old rubber *welts* to keep his shoes dry. (c) The *welts* on the girl's legs showed how severely she had been beaten. (d) The shoes are *welted* by a machine that stitches the uppers to the soles.

2. (a) Jane *excels* at all field sports. (b) The project was approved provided the cost did not *excel* fifty dollars. (c) We all praised the *excellence* of her cooking. (d) He has *excellent* taste in clothes.

3. (a) The huge sails *billowed* in the wind. (b) Great *billows* of smoke poured from the chimney. (c) A *billows* that stood in the fireplace was used to blow air into the fire to make it burn better. (d) The little boat was tossed about like a cork by the huge *billows* of the stormy sea.

4. (a) I brought back a *miniature* of the Statue of Liberty. (b) In the locket was a *miniature* of his wife, painted by himself. (c) It costs one dollar to ride on the *miniature* railroad. (d) The cut was quite *miniature*, but Mother insisted on putting a bandage on it.

5. (a) After a little while the storm began to *abyss*, and we were able to make our way home. (b) We stood at the edge of the *abyss* and looked down into its depths. (c) A great *abyss* separates the artist from his public. (d) The deepest part of the ocean is known as "the *abyss.*"

6. (a) He stayed at the gambling tables in a vain attempt to *recoup* his losses. (b) The police quickly *recouped* the prisoners who had escaped from the nearby jail. (c) She was full of plans for *recouping* her family's lost fortune. (d) They decided to rest for a few days in order to *recoup* their strength.

7. (a) The field of *staple* behind the barn will be ready for harvesting in a week or so. (b) We bought sugar, salt, flour, and other *staples.* (c) Coffee and bananas are the *staples* of Central America. (d) Automobile manufacturing is the *staple* industry of our economy.

8. (a) Spaceships will have to travel *immerse* distances to reach the other planets. (b) He was *immersed* in his studies, so I didn't disturb him. (c) I slowly *immersed* myself in the steaming water of the hot bath. (d) The steel

bars are cleaned by *immersion* in acid baths.

9. (a) He *writhed* in shame when his secret was discovered. (b) With a last desperate *writhe*, she freed herself of the rope. (c) She was *writhing* in agony when we got to her. (d) Smiles of happiness *writhed* the faces of the children when they were taken to the party.

10. (a) He was *deprived* of all his possessions and sent into exile. (b) Many English words are *deprived* from Latin and Greek. (c) I hope your cold will not *deprive* us of the pleasure of your company. (d) A person found guilty of treason may be *deprived* of his citizenship.

11. (a) If you expect me to believe that story, you must think me very *naive*. (b) He *naived* her of all her money and then left. (c) "I'm going to Hollywood to become a movie star," Lee said *naively*. (d) She is not as *naive* as she leads you to believe.

12. (a) The blade of the *tumbrel* fell with a swishing sound and chopped off the unlucky man's head. (b) The crowd gathered to witness the execution fell silent as the *tumbrel* bearing the prisoners approached. (c) The *tumbrel* returned empty to the prison after the guillotine had done its grim work. (d) The prisoners were herded into the *tumbrel* and driven to their execution.

13. (a) He led me up a flight of *rickety* steps to a small bedroom. (b) She drove up in a *rickety* drawn by two tired-looking horses. (c) The children's legs were *rickety* from the lack of proper nutrients in their food. (d) The building was very *rickety* and creaked and swayed alarmingly in the wind.

14. (a) For supper we had fried *scruple* with potatoes and apple rings. (b) The king did not *scruple* to punish those who had betrayed him. (c) Religious *scruples* forced him to turn down the offer of a post as assistant to the bishop. (d) She had no *scruples* about taking credit for something she had not done.

15. (a) Anyone who dares to whisper during a performance of the opera is *stigmatized* as a person of low breeding. (b) He was *stigmatized* as a thief for the rest of his life because of a foolish prank in his youth. (c) His eyes have begun to *stigmatize*, but he refuses to wear glasses. (d) Some critics have *stigmatized* America's material prosperity as nothing more than machine-worship.

16. (a) Daily exercise is the best way to keep your body *supple*. (b) Her drawings are noted for their *suppleness* of line. (c) After we had fed and *suppled* the horses, we retired to the inn. (d) Leather can be kept *supple* by regular polishing.

EXERCISE 4C

Rewrite each of the sentences below, replacing the italicized word or phrase with a word from Word List 4 and writing the word in the form that fits the rest of the sentence. Use each word only once. Write your answers in the spaces provided.

1. You will be *given a bad name* for the rest of your life if you are caught stealing, and you are *foolishly simple* to think otherwise.

.... stigmatized ....

.... naive ....

2. Because of her gambling, she was *allowed to have no part* of her allowance and so was not able to *win back* the money she had lost.

.... deprived ....

.... recoup ....

3. Cotton and rice are the *chief products* of my country.

.... staples ....

....

4. If she is *able to move her body easily*, there is

22

no reason why she shouldn't *do very well* as a dancer.

.... Supple ....

.... excel ....

5. She had no *feelings of guilt* about lying, but she *suffered great emotional discomfort* when she was found out.

.... Scruples ....

.... writhed ....

6. Across the *deep crack in the earth,* the natives had built a bridge that looked *as though it were about to fall down* but which was really quite safe.

.... abyss ....

.... rickety ....

7. I own a *very small portrait* of the queen of France that was worn by the king during his ride in the *cart that carried prisoners to their execution during the French Revolution.*

.... miniature ....

.... tumbrel ....

8. The bootmaker held the shoe in his lap and was *deeply absorbed* in the task of stitching the *leather strap that joins the sole to the upper.*

.... immersed ....

.... welt ....

9. Huge *swelling masses* of smoke poured from the burning building.

.... billows ....

....

An ABYSS is a deep crack or gap in the earth; the word has also come to refer to anything that is too deep to measure (*abysmal* ignorance). This secondary meaning becomes obvious when we examine the word. It is formed from the Greek word *byssos* (bottom) and the Greek prefix *a-* (written *an-* before vowels and the letter *h*), which means "without" or "not."

By combining this prefix with roots formed from the Greek words below, construct words that match each of the definitions given. Check each word in your dictionary for spelling and correctness.

1. *aisthesis* (feeling)
   partial or total loss of the sense of pain brought about by a drug or gas

   ....

2. *onoma* (name)
   given or written by one whose name is not known or is withheld

   ....

3. *mnasthai* (to remember)
   partial or total loss of memory

   ....

4. *theos* (god)
   one who believes that there is no God

   ....

5. *haima* (blood)
   condition in which a person's blood does not have enough red corpuscles and is unable to carry a normal amount of oxygen

   ....

6. *homos* (the same)
   anything that departs from the normal or usual

....

7. *morphe* (shape)
   not having a definite form or shape

....

8. *pathos*
   lack of emotion or of strong feelings; lack of interest

....

EXERCISE 4E

Write out, in the spaces provided, the words from Word List 4 for which a definition, homonym, synonym, or antonym is given below. When you are asked to give a root or a prefix, you should refer back to the preceding exercise; the information you require will be found there. Make sure that each of your answers has the same number of letters as there are spaces. A definition followed by a number is a review word; the number gives the Word List from which it is taken.

If all the words are filled in correctly, the boxes running up and down the answer spaces will continue the quotation begun earlier.

1. a great, deep crack in the earth's surface

2. an antonym for *sturdy*

3. a Greek prefix meaning "without"

4. to take away from; to dispossess

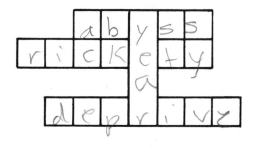

5. a synonym for *qualm*

6. careful in making up one's mind (1)

7. weak or feeble from sickness or old age (2)

8. to be better or greater in a certain way

9. without end; ceaseless (3)

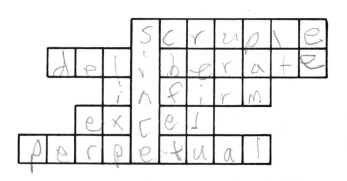

10. an antonym for *experienced*

24

11. a large ocean wave

12. a mark or ridge raised on the skin, as by a whip

13. an antonym for *lose*

14. to give a bad name to

15. to plunge into a liquid

16. an antonym for *stiff*

17. reduced in size; very small

18. a cart used during the French Revolution

19. an item of food used regularly and kept in stock

20. having to do with a horse or horses (2)

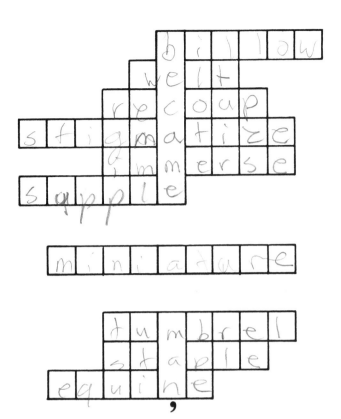

WORDLY WISE 4

ABYSS is pronounced *a-BISS*.

NAIVE is pronounced *ny-EVE*.

TUMBREL may also be spelled *tumbril*. The rolling of the *tumbrel* brought fear into the hearts of noblemen during the French Revolution, for this was the cart that carried prisoners to their execution. Its destination was the guillotine (pronounced *GEE-yo-teen* in French, *GIL-a-teen* in English), a machine for chopping off the heads of those sentenced to death.

Word List 5

ATROCITY	LIVID	STUPEFY
DESPOT	NOMAD	THESIS
DIEHARD	RUBBLE	VICTUALS
IMPUNITY	SHEER	WIGWAM
INTERMINABLE	STREW	

Look up the words above in your dictionary. Note that some of the words have more than one meaning. When you feel that you know *all* the meanings of *all* the words, go on to the following exercise.

EXERCISE 5A

From the four choices under each phrase or sentence, you are to mark the one that is closest in meaning to the word appearing in italics. When the same word appears more than once, you should note that it is being used in a different sense.

1. an *interminable* wait
(a) brief (b) endless (c) between trains (d) between performances

2. Who committed this *atrocity?*
(a) error (b) theft (c) injustice (d) terrible crime

3. Prepare the *victuals.*
(a) witnesses (b) food (c) medicine (d) reports

4. These people are *nomads.*
(a) wanderers from place to place (b) performers at circuses (c) highly skilled workers (d) bandits wanted by the law

5. to fear the *despot*
(a) powerful enemy (b) crowd's disapproval (c) wild animal (d) unjust ruler

6. an old *diehard*
(a) noble gentleman (b) soldier (c) wealthy

25

landowner (d) stubborn person

7. She finished her *thesis*.
(a) remarks before an audience (b) play set to music (c) long, researched essay (d) short novel

8. What is his *thesis*?
(a) address (b) excuse (c) answer (d) main idea

9. He robs with *impunity*.
(a) no fear of punishment (b) great skill and daring (c) no help from anyone (d) no thought for his victims

10. *sheer* stockings
(a) dark (b) tan (c) fine (d) heavy

11. *sheer* nonsense
(a) complete (b) partly (c) deliberate (d) easily misunderstood

12. The sides are *sheer*.
(a) rough (b) slippery (c) crumbling (d) steep

13. to *sheer* to the side
(a) look (b) swerve (c) turn (d) hurry

14. Don't *strew* those leaves!
(a) burn (b) rake (c) play in (d) scatter

15. We were *stupefied*!
(a) annoyed (b) pleased (c) excited (d) amazed

16. The drug *stupefied* her.
(a) excited (b) depressed (c) revived (d) dazed

17. He was *livid*.
(a) well-liked (b) ruddy faced (c) blue with cold (d) pale with rage

18. Her shoulder was *livid*.
(a) knocked out of joint (b) badly cut (c) black and blue (d) greatly improved

19. Clear away the *rubble*.
(a) piles of leaves (b) rubbish (c) broken bricks and stone (d) coarse sand

Check your answers against the correct ones below. The answers are not in order; this is to prevent your eye catching sight of the correct ones before you have had a chance to do the exercise on your own.

10c. 8d. 6d. 3b. 14d. 4a. 19c. 12d. 18c. 17d. 11a. 1b. 7c. 9a. 2d. 15d. 13b. 5d. 16d.

Go back to your dictionary and look up again those words for which you gave incorrect answers. Only after doing this should you go on to the next exercise.

EXERCISE 5B

Each word in Word List 5 is used four times in the sentences below; one of the sentences in each group uses the word incorrectly. You are to circle the letter that precedes that sentence. Do not circle more than one letter in any one group.

1. (a) Members of the nation gathered for a *wigwam* to decide whether or not to plant extra corn. (b) The *wigwam* was the dome or cone shaped home of the Native Americans of the Great Lakes region. (c) Since the Native American population is no longer so centralized, the art of making *wigwams* has largely been lost. (d) *Wigwams* were permanent homes, strongly made and covered with bark or hides.

2. (a) In her novel Uncle Tom's Cabin, Harriet Beecher Stowe describes the *atrocious* treatment meted out to slaves in the Old South. (b) As the old man neared the age of ninety, his muscles began to *atrocity*. (c) The deliberate killing of the prisoners was an *atrocity* that caused loud protests. (d) Each side in the war accused the other of the most terrible *atrocities*.

3. (a) He will receive his degree as soon as his *thesis* is accepted. (b) Professor Mosconi complained that she had four *theses* to read before the weekend. (c) Whose *thesis* was it that we hold the dance in the school gym? (d) The writer advances the *thesis* that all wars are caused by man's competitive instinct.

4. (a) Her face was *livid* with rage when she saw what I had done. (b) He flew into a *livid* when

26

he saw how he had been fooled. (c) I was shocked when I saw the *livid* bruise where the stone had hit him. (d) The skin around her eye was a *livid* purple.

5. (a) Joseph Stalin was one of a long line of Russian *despots*. (b) The queen began to *despot* her subjects as soon as she succeeded to the throne. (c) After ten years of *despotic* rule, he was finally overthrown. (d) Too much law in a *despotism* against which people revolt.

6. (a) Only an extreme *diehard* would fail to support this law. (b) We expect everyone to support the new policy except for a few *diehards*. (c) She tried to *diehard* her supporters into voting for the new measure. (d) He was a *diehard* politician, very hard to persuade.

7. (a) We picked our way through the *rubble*, trying to salvage what we could. (b) *Rubble* was spread along the roadbed and concrete poured over it. (c) The bombing had reduced most of the house to *rubble*. (d) I was *rubbling* through an old trunk in the attic when I found this.

8. (a) She wore a *stupefied* look, as though she had just been awakened from sleep. (b) We were *stupefied* by the news of our leader's death. (c) He fell into a *stupefy* from which nothing could awaken him. (d) The drug *stupefied* the elephant, enabling the veterinarian to remove the diseased tooth.

9. (a) "As long as you've *victuals* on your table and a roof over your head, you have nothing to worry about," the old man said. (b) They grew a few *victuals* in the garden at the back of the house. (c) They served cakes and pastries, but no substantial *victuals*. (d) They calculated they had *victuals* for two weeks and water for a little longer.

10. (a) These people *nomad* to the south in winter and return north in the spring. (b) The land was settled by *nomadic* people from the European plains. (c) He had led a somewhat *nomadic* life in his youth, but settle down when he got married. (d) The *nomads* wandered freely in search of fresh pasture for their livestock.

11. (a) She thought she could break the law with *impunity*, but she was mistaken. (b) One of the robbers was promised *impunity* from arrest provided she cooperated with the police. (c) Growing boys seem able to eat almost anything with *impunity*. (d) the police are so strict that a person cannot even jaywalk with *impunity*.

12. (a) Mother told us to tidy our room when she saw the clothes *strewn* on the floor. (b) I was very angry when I saw the two boys *strewing* stones at a little dog. (c) "With flowers thy bridal bed I *strew*." (d) The visitors continue to *strew* litter on the grass in spite of the receptacles provided.

13. (a) She decided that the stockings were not *sheer* enough. (b) The soldiers fled in *sheer* panic when they were attacked. (c) How long does it take a person to *sheer* a sheep? (d) The *sheer* face of the cliff offered no foothold.

14. (a) There were *interminable* discussions concerning the problems. (b) He talked *interminably* of his experience traveling in Italy. (c) He was a man of *interminable* years, anywhere from thirty-five to fifty. (d) After an *interminable* wait, we were finally admitted.

EXERCISE 5C

Rewrite each of the sentences below, replacing the italicized words or phrases with a word from Word List 5 and writing the word in the form that fits the rest of the sentence. Use each word only once. Write your answers in the spaces provided.

1. Her *long and carefully researched essay* deals at length with the habits of *people who lack a permanent home and travel constantly in search of pasture*.

. . . .

. . . .

2. We had enough fresh water and *food supplies* to last a week.

. . . .

. . . .

3. The Roman Emperor Nero committed all kinds of *wicked and terrible deeds,* with *no fear of being punished.*

. . . .

. . . .

4. The queen became *ashen-faced with rage* when she was accused of being a *cruel and unjust ruler.*

. . . .

. . . .

5. The bombing seemed *to go on forever,* and when it was finally over, the town had been reduced to *rough, broken pieces of stone and brick.*

. . . .

. . . .

6. They told me I was a *stubborn person who refuses to give up his opinions,* and I agreed with them.

. . . .

. . . .

7. I was *stricken senseless with amazement* when I looked over the edge and saw the *very steep* drop to the bottom.

. . . .

. . . .

8. Tell the children not to *scatter* the leaves all over the yard.

. . . .

. . . .

EXERCISE 5D

In Exercise 4D you learned that the Greek prefix *a-* or *an-* means "without" or "not." A very common Latin prefix, *in-* (which becomes *im-* before *b, m,* and *p*), has the same meaning and is generally used before roots of Latin origin. This prefix together with the Latin root *termin* (limit), gives us the word INTERMINABLE, which means "lasting; seeming to last forever." When combined with the Latin *poena* (punishment), it forms IMPUNITY, meaning "freedom from fear of punishment." Note that in this second example *in-* becomes *im-* before the *p*.

Change each of the following words into its opposite by adding the appropriate form of the prefix. Check each word in your dictionary for spelling and correctness.

1. ___VARIABLE

2. ___APPROPRIATE

3. ___MATURE

4. ___CAPABLE

5. ___PENITENT

6. ___FERTILE

7. ___PERSONAL

8. ___EFFECTIVE

9. ___MORTAL

10. ___ABILITY

11. ___ELEGANT

12. ___MOBILE

13. ___CURABLE

14. ___MODERATE

15. ___SENSITIVE

Using the root *termin*, which means "limit" or "end," complete the words below for which prefixes and suffixes have been supplied. Write out a brief definition of each word. Check each word and definition in your dictionary for accuracy.

16. _____A T E

. . . .

17. E X _____A T E

. . . .

18. _____A L

. . . .

19. D E _____E

. . . .

20. I N D E_____A T E

. . . .

EXERCISE 5E

Write out, in the spaces provided, the words from Word List 5 for which a definition, homonym, synonym, or antonym is given on the next page. When you are asked to give a root or a prefix, you should refer back to the preceding exercise; the information you require will be found there. Make sure that each of your answers has the same number of letters as there are spaces. A definition followed by a number is a review word; the number gives the Word List from which it is taken.

If all the words are filled in correctly, the boxes running up and down the answer spaces will continue the quotation begun earlier.

1. broken brick and stone

2. freedom from punishment or harm

3. a synonym for *food*

4. a cruel and wicked act

5. a person who will not change his views

6. discolored by bruising

7. a synonym for *tyrant*

8. an antonym for *brief*

9. a Latin prefix meaning "without"

10. a synonym for *scatter*

11. a Latin root meaning "limit"

12. a homonym for *shear*

13. pale with rage

14. a synonym for *amaze*

15. beaming (3)

16. the main idea, as of an argument or book

17. one who travels constantly in search of fresh pasture

18. an open insult (3)

WORDLY WISE 5

Immunity means "having protection against a disease"; a person may also be given *immunity* from being prosecuted for a crime. IMPUNITY means "without fear of punishment or harm." A person with *immunity* to smallpox may visit with *impunity* a person having the disease.

VICTUALS is a somewhat old-fashioned word that means "articles of food prepared for use." It is pronounced *vittles* and is sometimes spelled this way, although *victuals* is the preferred spelling.

Word List 6

CHASSIS	HURTLE	SACRED
CONTEMPORARY	INSPIRE	TERSE
ENTRAILS	OVERT	TREPIDATION
EPOCH	PRINCIPAL	WANE
HOVEL	PROW	WORTHLESS

Look up the words above in your dictionary. Note that some of the words have more than one meaning. When you feel that you know *all* the meanings of *all* the words, go on to the exercise below.

EXERCISE 6A

From the four choices under each phrase or sentence, you are to mark the one that is closest in meaning to the word appearing in italics. When the same word appears more than once, you should note that it is being used in a different sense.

1. an *overt* act
   (a) rude (b) open (c) sly (d) wicked

2. a *terse* statement
   (a) using more words than needed (b) using few words (c) expressing anger (d) expressing amusement

3. to *inspire* one's troops
   (a) give tasks to (b) give support to (c) arouse to action (d) speak affectionately of

4. entering a new *epoch*
   (a) tunnel through a mountain (b) partnership between two people (c) period of ten years (d) period in history

5. the *prow* of a boat
   (a) front (b) back (c) upper deck (d) lower deck

6. They live in a *hovel.*
   (a) shack (b) hotel (c) tent (d) apartment

7. *contemporary* paintings
   (a) expensive (b) good (c) modern (d) old

8. a *contemporary of* Queen Victoria
   (a) person writing a book on (b) person who lived at the same time as (c) person interested in the life of (d) portrait done during the life of

9. a broken *chassis*
   (a) machine for planting (b) automobile frame (c) wool-weaving machine (d) horse-drawn carriage

10. the *principal* parts
    (a) chief (b) only (c) removable (d) missing

11. the *principal* of the school
    (a) student body (b) guiding rule (c) person in charge (d) chief room

12. to pay back the *principal*
    (a) money borrowed (b) money stolen (c) person making the loan (d) bank or similar institution

13. a *worthless* picture
    (a) slightly damaged (b) stolen (c) valuable (d) valueless

14. Throw away the *entrails.*
    (a) parts that are spoiled (b) stones of plums or cherries (c) old newspapers and magazines (d) internal parts or guts of an animal

15. Our hopes *waned.*
    (a) grew stronger (b) were dashed (c) grew weaker (d) were justified

16. The car *hurtled* past.
    (a) rumbled noisily (b) moved very fast (c) moved silently (d) inched slowly

17. a look of *trepidation*
    (a) fear (b) hope (c) indifference (d) anger

18. *sacred* books
    (a) very old (b) religious (c) dull and boring (d) cheaply printed

19. a *sacred* promise
    (a) soon-forgotten (b) very serious (c) quickly broken (d) enforced

Check your answers against the correct ones below. The answers are not in order; this is to prevent your eye catching sight of the correct ones before you have had a chance to do the exercise on your own.

3c. 19b. 5a. 12a. 6a. 17a. 14d. 1b. 16b. 15c. 10a. 7c. 8b. 13d. 4d. 18b. 2b. 11c. 9b.

Go back to your dictionary and look up again those words for which you gave incorrect answers. Only after doing this should you go on to the next exercise.

EXERCISE 6B

Each word from Word List 6 is used four times in the sentences below; one of the sentences in each group uses the word incorrectly. You are to circle the letter that precedes that sentence. Do not circle more than one letter in any one group.

1. (a) My new job *entrails* a good deal of traveling. (b) The priests of Greek and Roman times claimed they could foretell the future by examining the *entrails* of birds. (c) The *entrails* of the slaughtered animals are made into pet food. (d) He cut open the body of the deer he had shot and removed the *entrails*.

2. She *hurtled* past me so fast that I barely glimpsed her face. (b) Why is everyone in such a *hurtle* these days? (c) I was surprised to learn that the earth is *hurtling* through space at over 20,000 miles per hour. (d) The subway *hurtles* hordes of workers daily into lower Manhattan.

3. (a) The library has copies of the Bible, the Talmud, and other *sacred* books. (b) The *sacred* was brought into church and laid on the altar. (c) This spot is *sacred* to the memory of those who fought and died here. (d) He made a *sacred* promise never to desert his leader.

4. (a) The fall of the Roman Empire in A.D. 476 was the end of an *epoch*. (b) James Watt was responsible for that *epoch*-making discovery, the steam engine. (c) Emily Brontë *epoched*

her novel **Wuthering Heights** in 1847. (d) Geologists give names to the different *epochs* of the earth's history.

5. (a) A line ran from the *prow* of the ship to the top of the mast. (b) The *prows* of old sailing ships were decorated with painted figureheads. (c) We saw the boat *prow* swiftly through the water. (d) The *prow* of the battleship cut cleanly through the water.

6. (a) The dollar today is more *worthless* than it was a few years ago. (b) He's a *worthless* fellow, and you should have nothing to do with him. (c) His ideas are *worthless* although he thinks of himself as a rather clever fellow. (d) If the painting is proved to be an imitation, it will be quite *worthless*.

7. (a) The *principal* of our high school has just retired after thirty years. (b) She objects on *principal* to children being forced to do things against their will. (c) Cotton was once the *principal* crop of the southern states. (d) If you cannot repay the *principal*, you will have to continue to pay interest.

8. (a) A look of *trepidation* crossed his face when he was told of the danger. (b) The thought of being left alone filled them with *trepidation*. (c) With great *trepidation* they entered the haunted house. (d) The *trepidation* seemed to be coming from the room above, so I went upstairs to investigate.

9. (a) The *terseness* of her answers led us to think she was a rude person. (b) "The answer is no!" she said *tersely*. (c) Keep the rope *terse* until I tell you to release it. (d) I received a very *terse* reply to my letter.

10. (a) Many works of genius were produced years ago, but many *contemporary* works will stand the test of time, as well. (b) Henry Wadsworth Longfellow and Walt Whitman were *contemporaries*. (c) Are you looking for *contemporary* work, or for something permanent? (d) The author has put a number of *contemporary*

political figures in her novel.

11. (a) She ended the dance with a graceful *chassis* and bowed to the applauding spectators. (b) The car's body is lowered onto the *chassis* and bolted in place. (c) He has about six *chassis* of old cards in his backyard. (d) I rebuilt the *chassis* of the radio and put it into a new cabinet.

12. (a) The woman kept trying to improve the *hovel* that was her home. (b) The houses in this part of town are little more than *hovels*. (c) It seems wrong that these people should have to lead such a *hovel* existence. (d) These *hovels* should have been torn down years ago to make way for better housing.

13. (a) By blowing up buildings and performing other *overt* acts, the rebels hoped to bring down the government. (b) She lifted up the *overt* and peered inside. (c) His speech in the Senate was an *overt* attempt to ruin his opponent. (d) They are now doing *overtly* what they have long been doing in secret.

14. (a) The beauties of nature *inspired* him to write poetry. (b) Many people in the party *inspired* to the leadership. (c) Her bravery was an *inspiration* to us all. (d) the coach was able to *inspire* the team with confidence despite their losing streak.

15. (a) The actress lived in constant fear that her popularity would begin to *wane*. (b) The weatherwane is stuck and always points in the same direction. (c) Daylight was *waning* as we returned to the house. (d) The fishing is best when the moon is on the *wane*.

EXERCISE 6C

Rewrite each of the sentences below, replacing the italicized words or phrases with a word from Word List 6 and writing the word in the form that fits the rest of the sentence. Use each word only once. Write your answers in the spaces provided.

1. During the baseball season, he *put heart into* the whole team, but now that the people know he's retiring, his influence is beginning to *grow less and less*.

   .... inspired ....

   .... wane ....

2. I was filled with *fear and trembling* when I saw the car *moving with great speed* toward us.

   .... trepidation ....

   .... hurtle ....

3. The note from the bank was *very short and to the point* and said simply that the *sum of money owed* plus the interest would have to be paid within seven days.

   .... terse ....

   .... principal ....

4. The *framework of the car on which the body rests* is *of no value* if it is twisted out of shape.

   .... chassis ....

   .... worthless ....

5. Benjamin Franklin was a noted *person who lived during the time* of George Washington.

   .... Contemporary ....

   ....

6. The shot fired across the *front part of the boat* was an *open and public* attempt to force the crew to turn back.

   .... prow ....

   .... overt ....

7. The settlement of America marked a new *period of human history* and helped bring about the modern world.

.... *eproch*

5. _____ R I Z E

....

8. They made a *very serious* promise to tear down these *small, broken-down shacks* and replace them with decent houses.

.... *sacred*

.... *hovels*

The prefix *com-* becomes *con-* before the following letters: *c, d, g, j, n, q, s, t,* and *v*. It becomes *col-* before *l; cor-* before *r;* and in some cases is shortened to *co-.*

Complete each of the words below by adding the correct form of the prefix *com-*. Write out a brief definition of each word. Check each word and definition in your dictionary for accuracy.

9. We eat every part of the animal except the *intestines and other innards.*

.... *entrails*

....

6. ___ E X I S T

....

EXERCISE 6D

The Latin word for "time" is *tempus;* you may have seen this word in the phrase *tempus fugit,* which means "time flies." Combined with the Latin prefix *com-,* meaning "together," *tempus* forms the root *tempo* in the word CONTEMPORARY, which means "living or occurring at the same time."

Using the root *tempo,* complete the words below for which prefixes and suffixes have been supplied. Write out a brief definition of each word. Check each word and definition in your dictionary for accuracy.

7. _____ T A C T

....

8. _____ D E S C E N D

....

9. _____ P E T E

....

10. _____ L E A G U E

....

1. _____ R A R Y

....

11. ___ H E R E N T

....

2. _____ (no prefix or suffix)

....

12. _____ C O C T

....

3. E X _____ R A N E O U S L Y

....

13. _____ B I N E

....

4. _____ R A L

....

14. _____ C O R D

....

15. ＿＿S O L I D A T E

. . . .

EXERCISE 6E

Write out, in the spaces provided, the words from Word List 6 for which a definition, homonym, synonym, or antonym is given below. When you are asked to give a root or a prefix, you should refer back to the preceding exercise; the information you require will be found there. Make sure that each of your answers has the same number of letters as there are spaces. A definition followed by a number is a review word; the number gives the Word List from which it is taken.

If all the words are filled in correctly, the boxes running up and down the answer spaces will continue the quotation begun earlier.

1. the framework of an automobile

2. a synonym for *chief*

3. an antonym for *priceless*

4. a synonym for *era*

5. an antonym for *stern*

6. the inside parts of animals

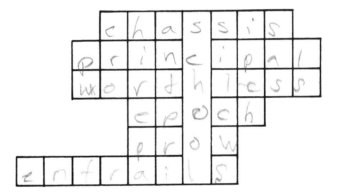

7. living or occurring in the same period

8. a synonym for *fear*

9. weak; shaky (4)

10. a synonym for *open*

11. having to do with religion; regarded as holy

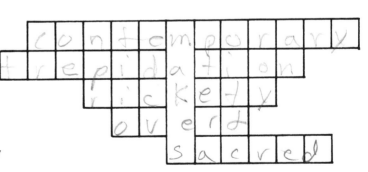

12. a synonym for *lessen*

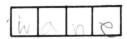

13. to cause, urge, or encourage to do something

14. a wretched house or hut

15. a Latin word meaning "time"

16. to steal money placed in one's keeping (2)

17. a synonym for *concise*

18. to move with great speed or force

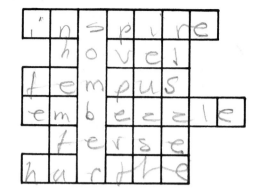

WORDLY WISE 6

CHASSIS comes to us from French and retains its original pronunciation, *SHAS-ee;* *CHAS-ee* is also correct. Note that the plural is spelled *chassis* also but is pronounced SHAS-*eez* or CHAS-*eez*.

To ask the *price* of something is to be told, usually, what it is *worth,* the two words being similar in meaning. However, WORTHLESS, far from being similar in meaning to *priceless,* is actually its antonym. *Worthless* means "without worth"; *priceless* suggests something so precious that it is beyond price and cannot be bought.

Don't confuse PRINCIPAL with its homonym *principle.* The difference between these two words is explained fully in Wordly Wise 7.

ACROSS

1. very small
11. a stubborn person
12. inexperienced; innocent
13. the main product of a country
15. a hut or shack
16. the forward part of a ship
17. most important; chief
20. bending easily
22. to plunge into a liquid
23. food
24. to outdo; to surpass
26. to make dull or senseless; daze
28. having to do with God or gods; holy
29. a large ocean wave
31. to give a bad name to
34. one who wanders from place to place
35. clear and to the point
37. to go, move, or slope back (3)
38. to spread about
41. open; public
42. rough, broken pieces of stone
45. black and blue
46. to arouse to action
47. existing at the same time
48. to pass or slip by (said of time) (1)
49. a long essay based on research

DOWN

2. lasting forever; endless
3. freedom from danger of punishment
4. fear; dread
5. to make up for losses
6. to get smaller or weaker
7. the organs inside an animal
8. an Indian tent
9. a mark or swelling on the skin
10. of or like a horse (2)
14. the framework of an automobile, television, etc.
18. weak and shaky
19. an absolute ruler; a tyrant
21. not easily disturbed (1)
25. to withhold something from
27. a cart used during the French Revolution
30. without value
31. extremely steep
32. not skilled; clumsy (1)
33. an act of great cruelty
36. an uneasy feeling; a misgiving
39. to twist and turn in pain or shame
40. to move or throw with great speed or force
43. a period of time in history
44. a deep crack in the earth

Chapter Three

Word List 7

ALTERNATE	MELEE	PARTICIPATE
CHRONIC	MINUTE	PRINCIPLE
COMPENSATE	OBLIQUE	SILT
ENTHRALL	OUTRAGE	SUMMON
FELON	PAGAN	WAX

Look up the words above in your dictionary. Note that some of the words have more than one meaning. When you feel that you know *all* the meanings of *all* the words, go on to the exercise below.

EXERCISE 7A

From the four choices under each phrase or sentence, you are to mark the one that is closest in meaning to the word appearing in italics. When the same word appears more than once, you should note that it is being used in a different sense.

1. a *minute* insect
   (a) very tiny (b) poisonous (c) many-legged (d) flying

2. a *minute* examination
   (a) brief (b) thorough (c) hurried (d) careless

3. Where are the *minutes*?
   (a) records of a meeting (b) persons attending a meeting (c) rules for conducting a meeting (d) membership lists

4. Please *alternate*.
   (a) listen (b) leave (c) take turns (d) try

5. Is there an *alternate*?
   (a) extra source of power (b) special reason (c) person who can take over (d) reply to a request

6. on *alternate* Tuesdays
   (a) all (b) any (c) every second (d) every third

7. a *principle* of democracy
   (a) important truth (b) serious fault (c) brief history (d) complete absence

8. the *principle* of the steam engine
   (a) chief part (b) chief use (c) underlying idea (d) wasted power

9. a man of *principle*
   (a) good taste (b) wisdom (c) honesty (d) noble birth

10. The moon *waxes*.
    (a) grows smaller (b) grows fuller (c) turns (d) shines

11. Cover it with *wax*.
    (a) a heavy, coarse cloth (b) a yellow, greasy substance (c) a hard, coarse rug (d) strong, thick paper

12. Did you *participate*?
    (a) take part (b) have fun (c) lead the way (d) explain

13. to *summon* the jury
    (a) send away (b) send for (c) instruct (d) question

14. *chronic* illness
    (a) mild (b) severe (c) widespread (d) long-lasting

15. a *pagan* tribe
    (a) constantly at war (b) moving from place to place (c) ruled by a single powerful person (d) worshiping many gods

16. It was an *outrage*.
    (a) secret way out (b) wicked act (c) silly trick (d) record

17. the *outraged* parents
    (a) angered (b) surprised (c) amused (d) sensible

18. *silt* left by the floods
    (a) wreckage (b) driftwood (c) fine sand (d) seaweed

19. an *oblique* line
    (a) curved (b) slanting (c) broken (d) double

20. an *oblique* suggestion
    (a) insulting (b) indirect (c) foolish (d) sensible

21. He is a *felon*.
    (a) criminal (b) sportsman (c) sick person (d) tyrant

22. to be involved in the *melee*
    (a) army operation (b) long march (c) celebration (d) noisy fight

23. We will *compensate* you.
    (a) hire (b) notify (c) interview (d) pay

24. This will *enthrall* the children.
    (a) fascinate (b) frighten (c) annoy (d) satisfy

Check your answers against the correct ones below. The answers are not in order; this is to prevent your eye catching sight of the correct ones before you have had a chance to do the exercise on your own.

17a. 3a. 15d. 11b. 5c. 9c. 24a. 22d. 8c. 2b. 20b. 14d. 6c. 18c. 12a. 21a. 16b. 23d. 10b. 1a. 19b. 7a. 13b. 4c.

Go back to your dictionary and look up again those words for which you gave incorrect answers. Only after doing this should you go on to the next exercise.

EXERCISE 7B

Each word from Word List 7 is used four times in the following sentences; one of the sentences in each group uses the word incorrectly. You are to circle the letter that precedes that sentence. Do not circle more than one letter in any one group.

1. (a) The fish lay their eggs in the *silty* bed of the sea. (b) The river bottom *silts* up quite quickly. (c) We *silted* through the rubble, looking for anything of value. (d) *Silt* is finer than sand and coarser than mud.

2. (a) Fists flying, we leaped into the *melee*. (b) In such a *melee* it was impossible to see which side was winning. (c) The fight between the two girls developed into a *melee* in which everyone took part. (d) They hid in a tree, hoping to *melee* the first traveler who passed beneath them.

3. (a) In case I can't accept, I have named you as my *alternate*. (b) The two actors will *alternate* in the role of Hamlet. (c) The street market is held on *alternate* Tuesdays. (d) We have no *alternate* but to press on with our plans.

4. (a) "Get out of my house!" she *outraged*. (b) The bombing of Pearl Harbor was an *outrage* to all Americans. (c) He lied *outrageously* when the police questioned him. (d) The price of meat is *outrageous* these days.

5. (a) He *waxed* the ends of his mustache to make them stick out. (b) She *waxed* angry when her request was turned down. (c) In the cage at the zoo were a fox with his *waxen* and two little cubs. (d) The moon *waxes* until it is full, and then it begins to wane.

6. (a) Easter, which is now observed by Christians, was once a *pagan* holiday. (b) The tribesmen gave up their *pagan* beliefs and were converted to Christianity. (c) The volcano was believed to be *pagan* by the natives who lived on the island. (d) The worship of *pagan* gods was an important part of the lives of the ancient Greek and Roman people.

7. (a) The king gave orders that all the *enthralls* imprisoned in his dungeons were to be released. (b) The audience was *enthralled* by the play. (c) Most of the spectators found the game the most *enthralling* of the season. (d) The old sea captain's tales of life at sea *enthralled* his young listeners.

8. (a) For my class talk I discussed the *principle* of the steam engine. (b) She is a woman of *principle*, and you may depend upon her word.

(c) She objects on *principle* to young people's buying of things they cannot afford. (d) My *principle* objection to him is that he doesn't get along with young people.

9. (a) She *summoned* up the amounts and gave us the total. (b) The president *summoned* his Cabinet for an urgent meeting. (c) We *summoned* up all our strength for one last effort. (d) I was *summoned* to appear in court on Monday morning.

10. (a) We ignored his grumbling, since we knew him to be a *chronic* complainer. (b) He has a touch of *chronic* and has been confined to his bed for a few days. (c) She suffers from a *chronic* disease of the lungs. (d) This new treatment is a boon to *chronic* sufferers from asthma.

11.
(a) He *obliqued* that he knew more about the matter than he was saying. (b) She suggested *obliquely* that it was time to leave. (c) An *oblique* triangle is one without a right angle. (d) The artist began by drawing an *oblique* line across the paper.

12.
(a) Are you *participating* in the school play? (b) The money was *participated* equally among those who had applied. (c) We all *participated* in the preparations for the party. (d) I want to see all the *participants* in the affair.

13. (a) Armed robbery is a *felony* punishable by up to twenty years in jail. (b) Among the first settlers in Australia were *felons* transported from England. (c) He was accused of trying to *felon* large sums of money that had been entrusted to his care. (d) A *felony* is a more serious crime than a misdemeanor.

14. (a) Many blind people have very good hearing, partially to *compensate* for their loss of sight. (b) We offered to *compensate* the farmer for any damage we might have caused. (c) *Compensation* will be paid to those suffering any loss. (d) I offered to *compensate* the money I owed her as soon as I was able.

15. (a) At one time it seemed impossible for anyone to run a mile in under four *minutes*. (b) The secretary read the *minutes* of the last meeting. (c) The *minute*, a slow and stately dance, was very popular in the seventeenth and eighteenth centuries. (d) Not even the *minutest* detail had been overlooked.

EXERCISE 7C
Rewrite each of the sentences below, replacing the italicized word or phrase with a word from Word List 7 and writing the word in the form that fits the rest of the sentence. Use each word only once. Write your answers in the spaces provided.

1. The doctor told the woman that her illness was *going to go on for a long time*.

. . . .

. . . .

2. She *gave orders for someone to call* her secretary so that *notes to provide a record of what was said at the meeting* could be taken down.

. . . .

. . . .

3. The historian devoted two chapters of his book to the *people of ancient Rome who believed in many gods*.

. . . .

. . . .

4. The manager made a *somewhat indirect* suggestion that the teenagers and the younger children *take turns with each other* in using the swimming pool.

. . . .

. . . .

5. Following the floods, the owners agreed to

remove the *fine sandy deposits left by the water* but not to *make up for any losses suffered by* the people living in the houses.

. . . .

. . . .

6. I hope you did not *take part* in the *noisy brawl* that broke out.

. . . .

. . . .

7. I always thought of him as a man of *honesty and fair dealing,* but his attempt to cheat you is an *act of great wickedness.*

. . . .

. . . .

8. The children were *gripped with excitement* as the old sea captain told them of his voyages.

. . . .

. . . .

9. He grew more and more angry when accused of being a *person who has been convicted of a serious crime.*

. . . .

. . . .

EXERCISE 7D

From the Greek *chronos,* "time," comes our word CHRONIC, which means "lasting a long time." You may remember from Exercise 6D that the Latin word for time is *tempus.* Both of these roots are found in a number of English words.

Complete each of the sentences below with the appropriate word that has *chron* or *chrono* as its root. Two of the words require prefixes and these have been supplied.

1. This chart contains the main events in American history arranged in . . . . order.

2. The workers taking part in the operation were told to syn . . . . their watches so that they would all act at the same time.

3. A . . . . play deals with historical events that occur over a long period of time.

4. A . . . . is a more accurate timekeeper than an ordinary watch.

5. The striking of a clock in Shakespeare's play **Julius Caesar** would be an ana . . . . since there were no clocks in Caesar's time.

Write out below the five words you used to complete the above sentences. Give a brief definition for each. Check the spelling and correctness of each word in your dictionary.

6. *word* . . . .

   definition . . . .

7. *word* . . . .

   definition . . . .

8. *word* . . . .

   definition . . . .

9. *word* . . . .

   definition . . . .

10. *word* . . . .

   definition . . . .

EXERCISE 7E

Write out, in the spaces provided, the words from Word List 7 for which a definition, homonym, synonym, or antonym is given below. When you are asked to give a root or a prefix, you should refer back to the preceding exercise; the information you require will be found there. Make sure that each of your answers has the same number of letters as there are spaces. A definition followed by a number is a review word; the number gives the Word List from which it is taken.

If all the words are filled in correctly, the boxes running up and down the answer spaces will continue the quotation begun earlier.

1. one who believes in more than one god

2. an antonym for *bore*

3. to take turns regularly

4. a deep crack in the earth's surface (4)

5. to make up for; to pay for any losses

6. an antonym for *wane*

7. an act of great wickedness

8. to take part with others; to join in

9. an antonym for *brief*

10. a synonym for *indirect*

11. a synonym for *rule*

12. a Greek root meaning "time"

13. an antonym for *huge*

14. fine particles of sand deposited by water

15. an essay presented by a candidate for an academic degree (5)

16. a synonym for *brawl*

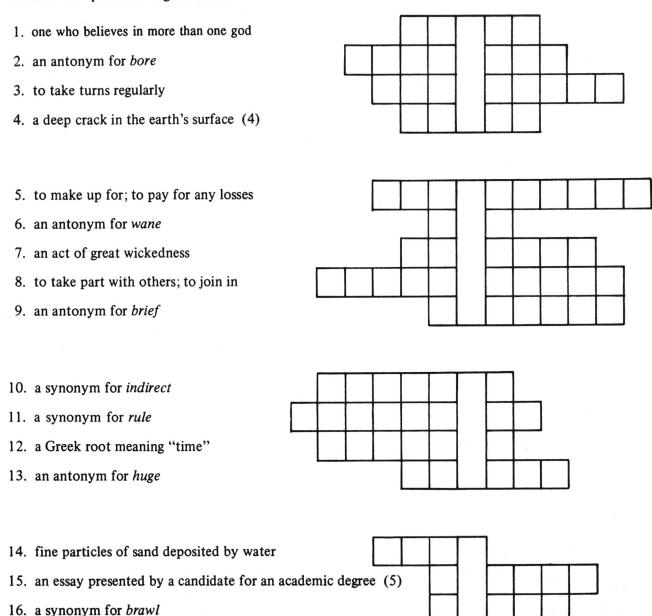

WORDLY WISE 7

ALTERNATE is pronounced *OL–turn–it* when it means "every other" (as *alternate* Thursdays), and when it means "a substitute" or "a person to replace someone." It is pronounced *OL–tur–nate* when it means "to take turns." Don't confuse this word with *alternative* which means "a choice."

Medley (as in the phrase "a medley of songs") means "mixture"; the word comes from the Old French *medlee* (a mixing). From this same source, with the *d* dropped in the process, comes our word MELEE (pronounced *MAY-lay* or *may-LAY* to show its French origin) for a mixing of a different kind—"a confused, hand-to-hand brawl."

MINUTE is pronounced *MIN–it* when it refers to a period of time of 60 seconds, or to the records of a meeting. In its other meanings it is pronounced *my–NEWT*.

PAGAN is a word that once filled a need, but is now coming to the end of its usefulness, except in a historical context. A hundred years ago, Christian missionaries tried to convert people they called pagan or *heathen* (the two words being used interchangeably). Whole societies, in Asia and Africa particularly, were called pagan because their religions were other than the dominant ones of the Jewish, Christian, and Moslem faiths. Today we are much more accepting of differing religious beliefs. As a result of this change in attitude, the word *pagan* is generally restricted now to the people of the ancient world, Romans and Greeks, who worshiped many gods and who lived before the rise of the three great religions of the modern world that worshiped a single god.

Word List 8

ARENA	INTERMITTENT	RECOLLECT
CONCISE	OASIS	RELUCTANT
DETERMINE	ONSLAUGHT	SEDENTARY
ESTUARY	PAMPER	SHEAR
INFALLIBLE	PAWN	TENSE

Look up the words above in your dictionary. Note that some of the words have more than one meaning. When you feel that you know *all* the meanings of *all* the words, go on to the exercise below.

EXERCISE 8A

From the four choices under each phrase or sentence, you are to mark the one that is closest in meaning to the word appearing in italics. When the same word appears more than once, you should note that it is being used in a different sense.

1. Our teacher seems *infallible*.
   (a) friendly (b) unable to remember anything (c) quick to get angry (d) never to make a mistake

2. *intermittent* sounds
   (a) unpleasant (b) stopping and starting (c) distant (d) heard only by dogs

3. We crossed the *estuary*.
   (a) small stream (b) range of mountains (c) place where railroad tracks meet (d) place where a large river meets the sea

4. a *concise* report
   (a) long and boring (b) carefully prepared (c) short and clear (d) political

5. to *determine* to go
   (a) want badly (b) ask politely (c) make up one's mind (d) refuse over and over

6. to *determine* the amount
   (a) offer (b) figure out (c) receive (d) forget

7. a large *arena*
   (a) sheep ranch (b) place for contests (c) private garden (d) Indian reservation

8. the wrong *tense*
   (a) noun form showing position (b) agreement between subject and verb (c) agreement between adjective and noun (d) verb form showing time.

9. She is always *tense*.
   (a) joking (b) active (c) nervous (d) willing to help

10. Is the rope *tense?*
    (a) about to break (b) strong enough (c) stretched tightly (d) starting to slip

11. Don't *pamper* the child.
    (a) tease (b) give in to (c) keep up late (d) scold

12. She was most *reluctant*.
    (a) unwilling (b) encouraging (c) helpful (d) annoying

13. We stopped at the *oasis*.
    (a) small cabin in the mountains (b) large hotel in the city (c) small clearing in the forest (d) watering place in the desert

14. to *recollect* the details
    (a) remember (b) forget (c) write out (d) leave out

15. to *shear* off the edges
    (a) burn (b) break (c) chop (d) cut

16. to *shear* a sheep
    (a) kill (b) cut up (c) clip the wool off (d) mark with a dye

17. Many were killed in the *onslaught*.
    (a) plane crash (b) flood (c) fierce attack (d) fire

18. She lost her *pawn*.
    (a) large pocket watch (b) small amount of money (c) pin made of gold or silver (d) minor chess piece

19. He is just a *pawn*.
    (a) messenger (b) petty thief (c) ordinary foot soldier (d) person used by others

20. to *pawn* a watch
    (a) buy very cheaply (b) leave in exchange for a loan (c) damage beyond repair (d) give as a prize.

21. a *sedentary* worker
    (a) very slow (b) careless (c) who sits (d) who uses his hands

Check your answers against the correct ones above. The answers are not in order; this is to prevent your eye catching sight of the correct ones before you have had a chance to do the exercise on your own.

44

Go back to your dictionary and look up again those words for which you gave incorrect answers. Only after doing this should you go on to the next exercise.

EXERCISE 8B

Each word from Word List 8 is used four times in the sentences below; one of the sentences in each group uses the word incorrectly. You are to circle the letter that precedes that sentence. Do not circle more than one letter in any one group.

1. (a) After studying the board carefully, he moved his *pawn* next to my queen. (b) She was a willing *pawn* of those who had plotted her country's overthrow. (c) He was so poor that he had to *pawn* his violin to buy food. (d) She looked so *pawn* that I suggested she lie down for a while.

2. (a) A high stone wall around the house *determined* people from entering the grounds. (b) A boy's hobby often *determines* his choice of a career. (c) The cause of the accident has not yet been *determined*. (d) She was *determined* to succeed.

3. (a) The native chief spoke to us in *infallible* English. (b) No system is completely *infallible*, but this one comes close. (c) He has an *infallible* method of finding out the sex of a chick before it has hatched. (d) Her air of *infallibility* annoyed everyone.

4. (a) We were totally unprepared for the sudden *onslaught* launched by the enemy. (b) The poor clerk wilted under the store owner's verbal *onslaught*. (c) Many brave men were *onslaughted* in the battle. (d) The enemy lacked the strength to withstand our terrific *onslaught*.

5. (a) He is *reluctant* to ask anyone for help. (b) We used a very strong *reluctant* to glue the pieces together. (c) After *reluctant* farewells, we set out on our journey. (d) She agreed *reluctantly* to accompany us.

6. (a) The spaceship landed on the moon at the *concise* moment predicted by the scientists. (b) Please make your statement as *concise* as possible. (c) She achieves a *conciseness* in her writing without leaving out anything of importance. (d) You expressed yourself clearly and *concisely*.

7. (a) They dug an *oasis* in the sandy desert in the hope of striking water. (b) From the air the *oasis* was a speck of green in the middle of a vast, sandy wasteland. (c) There are very few *oases* in this part of the desert. (d) His home was an *oasis* of calm in a hectic and troubled world.

8. (a) Be kind to your children, but do not *pamper* them. (b) She led a very *pampered* existence as a child (c) A nail had *pampered* a hole in the tire. (d) You must *pamper* these plants, since they are very delicate and may die if not cared for properly.

9. (a) The cat *tensed* its muscles as it prepared to pounce. (b) The *tension* mounted as the play drew toward its close. (c) He *tensed* his teeth to prevent himself from crying out. (d) We had to write out the past and future *tenses* of the verb "to be."

10. (a) He was used to an outdoor life and disliked *sedentary* work. (b) He is a man of *sedentary* habits. (c) *Sedentary* workers need more exercise than those who work with their muscles. (d) The *sedentary* settles to the bottom, leaving a clear liquid.

11. (a) *Intermittent* fever is common in cases of malaria. (b) There will be *intermittent* rain during the afternoon and early evening. (c) The radio played *intermittently* all day. (d) There is a beginner's, an *intermittent*, and advanced class in each subject.

12. (a) It was *shear* luck that I happened to be passing at that moment. (b) She trimmed the hedges with a large pair of *shears*. (c) The entire fender was *sheared* off in the accident. (d) The sheep are *sheared* in the spring, and by winter the wool has grown again.

13. (a) At the end of the game he *recollected* the cards and shuffled them. (b) I'm trying to *recollect* the woman's name. (c) I have a faint *recollection* of seeing her once. (d) Do you *recollect* the words of that song we always used to sing?

14. (a) The water in the river has become very *estuary* and is no longer fit to drink. (b) The ship anchored in the *estuary*, waiting for the tide to turn. (c) We were very excited when the ship left the *estuary* and headed for the open sea. (d) The ferry across the *estuary* leaves every hour.

15. (a) The *arena* was sometimes flooded, and naval battles were fought for the enjoyment of the Roman crowds. (b) At the age of eighty the senator decided to retire from the political *arena*. (c) As the two boxers entered the *arena*, the spectators cheered wildly. (d) He examined every *arena* of the problem before making up his mind.

EXERCISE 8C

Rewrite each of the following sentences, replacing the italicized word or phrase with a word from Word List 8 and writing the word in the form that fits the rest of the sentence. Use each word only once. Write your answers in the spaces provided.

1. Here is a place where you can *get a loan by leaving with them* your watch and get it back when you repay the money.

.....pawn.........................

....

2. She is *not at all eager* to take her children to the circus because she does not like to *spoil them by doing too much for* them.

........reluctant..................

45

.... *pamper* ....

3. The crowd became *nervous and excited* as the two boxers entered the *place where the fight was to take place.*

.... dense ....

.... arena ....

4. Weather forecasters are not *incapable of making a mistake,* but they did say that showers would be *stopping and starting at intervals* all afternoon.

.... infallible ....

.... intermittent ....

5. The enemy soldiers crossed the *wide mouth of the river* under cover of darkness and began their *fierce attack* at dawn.

.... chronometer ....

....

6. The Australian rancher gave us a *brief and clear* description of how to *clip the wool from* a sheep.

.... chronism ....

....

7. I know we are near a *small, fertile place in the desert that has a supply of water,* but I cannot *bring to mind* its name.

.... chronological ....

....

8. I would like to *find out exactly* how much exercise a person needs whose work is *done mainly while he is sitting down.*

.... synchronize ....

EXERCISE 8D

The word INTERMITTENT means "stopping and starting again" and is made up of the Latin prefix *inter-* (between) and the root *mitt* (also written *mit* or *miss*) from the Latin *mittere* (to send).

Complete each of the words below, for which prefixes and suffixes have been supplied, by filling in the appropriate form of the root (*mitt, mit,* or *miss*). Write out a brief definition of each word, checking both word and definition in your dictionary for accuracy and spelling.

1. ____ I O N A R Y

....

2. ____ I V E

....

3. R E ____

....

4. E ____

....

5. C O M ____ I O N

....

6. S U B ____

....

7. C O M ____

....

8. P E R ____

....

9. D I S_____

10. T R A N S_____E R

. . . .

EXERCISE 8E

Write out, in the spaces provided, the words from Word List 8 for which a definition, homonym, synonym, or antonym is given below. When you are asked to give a root or a prefix, you should refer back to the preceding exercise; the information you require will be found there. Make sure that each of your answers has the same number of letters as there are spaces. A definition followed by a number is a review word; the number gives the Word List from which it is taken.

If all the words are filled in correctly, the boxes running up and down the answer spaces will conclude the quotation begun earlier.

1. an antonym for *rambling*

2. to remove (wool or hair) by cutting

3. an antonym for *erring*

4. a place set aside or used for fighting

5. to ride a horse at a slow gallop (2)

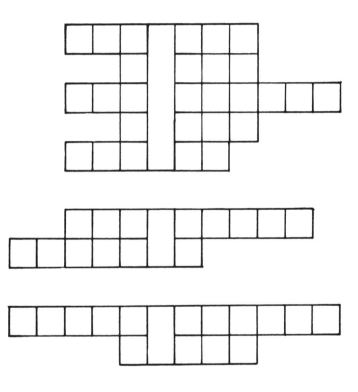

6. a synonym for *remember*

7. to amaze; to astonish (5)

8. stopping and starting at intervals

9. a nature goddess (1)

10. a fertile spot in a desert region

11. an antonym for *willing*

12. a synonym for *decide*

13. characterized by much sitting

14. a synonym for *indulge*

15. the tidal mouth of a river

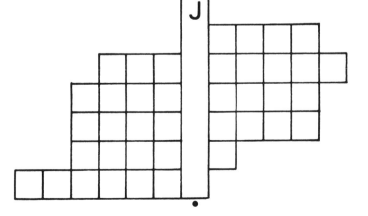

WORDLY WISE 8

A favorite sport of the people of ancient Rome was watching "contests" between unarmed or poorly armed men and ferocious lions and other wild beasts. Naturally, when the animals won, blood flowed freely at such events. Sand was strewn on the ground to soak up the blood, and the Latin word for sand, *harena,* came to be applied to such a place of battle and bloodshed. By dropping the *h* we have the English word ARENA.

When a river discharges water into the sea and meets the incoming tide of the ocean, there results a great deal of turbulence in the water. This fact must have been noted by the Romans, since our word for a wide, tidal river mouth, ESTUARY, comes from the Latin *aestuarium* which means "bubbling" or "boiling."

Don't confuse SHEAR with its homonym *sheer* (Word List 5). *Shear* is a verb and means (1) to cut as with scissors, (2) to clip the hair, wool, etc. from, (3) to move as if by cutting. (The boat *sheared* through the water.) *Sheer* is a verb and means "to turn aside" or "to swerve." It is also an adjective and means (1) very thin or fine, (2) absolute; utter, (3) straight up and down; very steep. *Sheer* may also be an adverb, meaning "altogether; completely."

Word List 9

BUSTLE	LEGIBLE	REFRAIN
DONATE	MEMORABLE	SCOUR
FINANCIAL	OPTIMIST	STATUTE
ILLUSTRIOUS	PRELIMINARY	STUPOR
IMPAIR	PRIM	SUCCINCT

Look up the words above in your dictionary. Note that some of the words have more than one meaning. When you feel that you know *all* the meanings of *all* the words, go on to the exercise below.

EXERCISE 9A

From the four choices under each phrase or sentence, you are to mark the one that is closest in meaning to the word appearing in italics. When the same word appears more than once, you should note that it is being used in a different sense.

1. She is an *optimist*.
   (a) eye doctor (b) cheerful person (c) person who makes glasses (d) disappointed person

2. a *succinct* reply
   (a) witty (b) vague (c) concise (d) inaudible

3. an *illustrious* painter
   (a) very famous (b) unknown (c) who illustrates books (d) long dead

4. *legible* handwriting
   (a) easy to read (b) sloppy (c) small and cramped (d) faded

5. in a *stupor*
   (a) rage (b) makeshift bed (c) hurry (d) daze

6. to *donate* $100
   (a) earn (b) save over a long period (c) spend foolishly (d) give to a cause

7. the *bustle* of traffic
   (a) noisy movement (b) increased volume (c) poisonous fumes (d) controlled flow

8. a skirt with a *bustle*
   (a) projecting, padded back (b) high waist (c) skirt that trails behind on the floor (d) hem that just touches the floor

9. the *preliminary* stages
   (a) awkward (b) final (c) early (d) most difficult

10. *financial* problems
    (a) trivial (b) boring (c) serious (d) money

11. an unfair *statute*
    (a) question (b) law (c) demand (d) condition

12. to *scour* the sink
    (a) install (b) scrub (c) scratch (d) remove

13. to *scour* the area
    (a) leave hurriedly (b) set fire to (c) improve (d) search thoroughly

14. a *memorable* visit
(a) long-remembered (b) soon-forgotten (c) hasty (d) pleasant

15. to *impair* one's eyes
(a) shade (b) correct (c) damage (d) examine

16. to *refrain* from speaking
(a) become tired (b) become thirsty (c) retire (d) hold back

17. a jolly *refrain*
(a) person who makes animal noises (b) children's song (c) group of singers (d) repeated phrase in a song

18. a *prim* person
(a) strong and healthy (b) tall and thin (c) stiffly formal (d) weak-minded

Check your answers against the correct ones below. The answers are not in order; this is to prevent your eye catching sight of the correct ones before you have had a chance to do the exercise on your own.

3a. 11b. 18c. 5d. 6d. 17d. 14a. 1b. 15c. 16d. 9c. 4a. 12b. 7a. 10d. 2c. 13d. 8a.

Go back to your dictionary and look up again those words for which you gave incorrect answers. Only after doing this should you go on to the next exercise.

EXERCISE 9B

Each word from Word List 9 is used four times in the following sentences; one of the sentences in each group uses the word incorrectly. You are to circle the letter that precedes that sentence. Do not circle more than one letter in any one group.

1. (a) Every *donation*, no matter how small, will be acknowledged. (b) I offered to *donate* some old clothes to the charity sale. (c) The pressure of work was the excuse she *donated* for her not coming to the meeting. (d) I have *donated* much time and effort to this project.

2. (a) He tried to *bustle* up his courage by whistling to himself. (b) He *bustled* about the office, trying to look busy. (c) Dresses with *bustles* were very popular at the end of the nineteenth century. (d) I enjoy the *bustle* of the city but love to escape to the country from time to time.

3. (a) Her terrible experiences in the war have *impaired* her reason. (b) He suffers from a serious *impair* of the liver. (c) Her eyesight is somewhat *impaired*, but the trouble can be easily corrected. (d) She had so many students that her own musical career was *impaired*.

4. (a) The chairman summed up the discussion most *succinctly*. (b) I would love to sink my teeth into a *succinct* steak right now. (c) "I came; I saw; I conquered," Caesar said *succinctly*. (d) Please make your reply as *succinct* as possible.

5. (a) The king met with his chief *statute* to discuss the new law. (b) This *statute* has been in the book for nearly two hundred years. (c) The *statutory* retiring age is sixty-five. (d) The *statute* book is the name given to the state's body of laws as a whole.

6. (a) Most of the books on display lacked pictures, but the ones I bought were *illustrious*. (b) Some of the most *illustrious* names in the theater were on the list. (c) Her *illustrious* accomplishments assure her of lasting fame. (d) He comes from one of the most *illustrious* families in the country.

7. (a) They were in a *stupor* from all the wine they had drunk. (b) This tablet will *stupor* him and put him to sleep. (c) He apologized for his *stupor*, but he explained that he had just taken a sleeping pill. (d) By this time we were in a *stupor* of mental weariness.

8. (a) The ink had faded so much that the writing was barely *legible*. (b) Only juniors and seniors are *legible* to sit on the student council. (c) Please write *legibly* so that I can read what you have written. (d) At ninety, she still wrote in a

49

bold and *legible* hand.

9. (a) The project will be *financialed* by a group of wealthy citizens. (b) The company is *financially* sound and has capable management. (c) A group of *financiers* from New York agreed to put up the money. (d) She put her *financial* affairs in order just before she died.

10. (a) He *optimisted* that things were bound to get better. (b) "I'm sure I'll win the money," she said *optimistically*. (c) Her *optimism* was based more on wishful thinking than on the facts of the situation. (d) He always takes an *optimistic* view of life.

11. (a) "I never speak to strangers," he said *primly*. (b) Her old-fashioned clothes gave her a somewhat *prim* appearance. (c) She *primmed* her lips in a straight line and refused to speak. (d) She was *prim* in her ways but quite friendly when you got to know her.

12. (a) A *preliminary* investigation failed to show anything wrong. (b) I greeted the *preliminaries* as they arrived for the meeting. (c) When the *preliminaries* were over, we got down to business. (d) After the *preliminary* bouts, the master of ceremonies announced the main fight of the evening.

13. (a) Our trip to Washington was made *memorable* by our glimpse of the president on the grounds of the White House. (b) She wrote a *memorable* to herself so that she would not forget. (c) The first book he wrote was his most *memorable* work. (d) She often referred to that *memorable* winter of 1912 when the snow was five feet deep.

14. (a) The organization has been completely *refrained* for this summer's camp. (b) Please *refrain* from whistling. (c) He had an impulse to say something but, on second thought, *refrained*. (d) Everyone who knew the words joined in the *refrain*.

15. (a) Sprinkle a little *scour* on the stain and rub it with a damp cloth. (b) He has agents *scouring* the country, looking for bright young people to join his company. (c) I *scoured* the pans with steel wool. (d) These boulders were left behind when the countryside was *scoured* by the glaciers during the Ice Age.

EXERCISE 9C
Rewrite each of the sentences below, replacing the italicized word or phrase with a word from Word List 9 and writing the word in the form that fits the rest of the sentence. Use each word only once. Write your answers in the spaces provided.

1. He is rather *formal and precise in manner* and disapproves strongly of the *noisy activity* of modern life.

   . . . .

   . . . .

2. We were told to keep our reports *short and to the point* and to make sure that our writing was *capable of being read*.

   . . . .

   . . . .

3. Since the organization's needs are mainly *to do with money*, we hope you will *make an offering of* ten dollars.

   . . . .

   . . . .

4. The evening was truly *one that we could never forget* because of the many *famous and outstanding* persons we met at the dinner.

   . . . .

   . . . .

5. The police have been told to enforce this *law which has been passed by the state government*.

. . . .

. . . .

6. I must *keep myself* from cheering because it might *weaken* my voice.

. . . .

. . . .

7. We *made a thorough search of* the neighborhood for the missing man and finally found him wandering about in a *confused state of mind.*

. . . .

. . . .

8. You must really be a *person who always looks on the bright side* if you think the *first part of the* work can be finished in a week.

. . . .

. . . .

EXERCISE 9D

This exercise reviews the roots and prefixes covered so far. Underline the prefix in each of the words below. Give the meaning of each prefix, and write out two words having the same prefix.

1. coherent . . . .

. . . .

. . . .

2. recede . . . .

. . . .

. . . .

3. antipathy . . . .

4. anonymous . . . .

. . . .

. . . .

Underline the root in each of the words below. Give the meaning of each root, and write out two words having the same root.

5. sociable . . . .

. . . .

. . . .

6. terminate . . . .

. . . .

. . . .

7. remit . . . .

. . . .

. . . .

8. chronometer . . . .

. . . .

. . . .

9. comprehend . . . .

. . . .

10. temporary . . . .

. . . .

Write out, in the spaces provided, the words from Word List 9 for which a definition, homonym, synonym, or antonym is given below. When you are asked to give a root or a prefix, you should refer back to the preceding exercise; the information you require will be found there. Make sure that each of your answers has the same number of letters as there are spaces. A definition followed by a number is a review word; the number gives the Word List from which it is taken.

If all the words are filled in correctly, the boxes running up and down the answer spaces will give the first four words of a riddle. The riddle will be continued in Exercise 10E.

1. to spread about; to scatter (5)

2. logically connected; clearly put together (1)

3. the tidal mouth of a river (8)

4. a synonym for *daze*

5. to twist and turn, as with pain (4)

6. to clean thoroughly by rubbing

7. a synonym for *concise*

8. a synonym for *readable*

9. characterized by much sitting (8)

10. an antonym for *unknown*

11. long remembered; remarkable

12. noisy or energetic activity

13. a synonym for *give*

14. an antonym for *final*

15. a noisy fight or brawl (7)

16. an antonym for *improve*

17. an antonym for *pessimist*

18. a rule or law passed by a governing body

19. having to do with money and its management

20. frail; weak (4)

21. a repeated phrase in a song

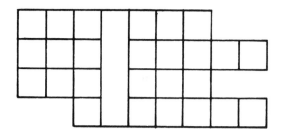

ACROSS

1. to give in to; to indulge
4. to grow weaker; to grow less (6)
6. short and clear
14. formal and precise in manner
15. a projecting padded piece on the back of a skirt
16. to send for
18. stopping and starting again
19. to cut with scissors
20. a person made use of by others
21. very famous
25. said in a few words; short
27. a noisy, confused fight
29. to decide; to settle
30. to hold back from doing something
32. to give, as to a charity
34. incapable of making mistakes
38. to take part in
40. stretched tight
44. the wide, tidal mouth of a river
45. a scientific law explaining how something works
46. a wicked act
47. a fierce attack
48. not wanting (to); unwilling
49. long-remembered; remarkable

DOWN

1. coming before the action
2. very small; tiny
3. to hold in a spell; to charm
5. anything owned that has value (2)
7. a fertile spot in a desert
8. to make up for; to repay
9. to clean thoroughly
10. a place set aside for fighting
11. freedom from punishment or harm (5)
12. slanting
13. a mark or ridge on the skin (4)
17. a person who always remains hopeful
22. easy to read; clear
23. to remember
24. characterized by much sitting
26. long-lasting
28. to grow stronger or larger
31. having to do with money
33. to take turns
35. a law passed by a governing body
36. lacking experience; childlike (4)
37. a dazed condition
39. to damage or weaken
41. a person convicted of a serious crime
42. **one who has little or no religion**
43. fine sand or mud

Chapter Four

Word List 10

ACCLAIM	FLIPPANT	OBSCENE
AQUATIC	HALTER	RECURRENCE
BELLIGERENT	INDISPOSED	TIMOROUS
BLIZZARD	MAZE	TWINGE
BONDAGE	MURKY	UNSCATHED
EXTENSIVE		

Look up the words above in your dictionary. Note that some of the words have more than one meaning. When you feel that you know *all* the meanings of *all* the words, go on to the exercise below.

EXERCISE 10A

From the four choices under each phrase or sentence, you are to mark the one that is closest in meaning to the word appearing in italics. When the same word appears more than once, you should note that it is being used in a different sense.

1. She was *unscathed.*
   (a) unafraid (b) unharmed (c) underfed (d) poorly clothed

2. I fastened the *halter.*
   (a) clip on a necklace (b) rope for leading an animal (c) gate of a corral (d) lock on a door

3. a *halter* to go with the skirt
   (a) woman's upper garment (b) broad, cloth-covered belt (c) matched set of shoes and purse (d) turbanlike hat

4. ten years in *bondage*
   (a) prison (b) exile (c) hiding (d) slavery

5. to *acclaim* the performer
   (a) admire (b) greet with loud applause (c) dismiss with loud booing (d) eagerly await

6. public *acclaim*
   (a) praise (b) property (c) disapproval (d) discussion

7. *aquatic* plants
   (a) desert (b) flowering (c) water (d) evergreen

8. *indisposed* to help
   (a) anxious (b) expecting (c) unwilling (d) required

9. He is *indisposed.*
   (a) very angry (b) very uncomfortable (c) slightly ill (d) rather bored

10. a *timorous* child
    (a) noisy (b) well-behaved (c) fearful (d) sick

11. *extensive* damage
    (a) slight (b) widespread (c) costly (d) irreparable

12. *extensive* changes
    (a) unexpected (b) long-awaited (c) necessary (d) far-reaching

13. *obscene* language
    (a) free-flowing (b) poetic (c) indecent (d) hard to understand

14. a *belligerent* gesture
    (a) generous (b) quarrelsome (c) friendly (d) unexpected

15. the *belligerent* nations
    (a) allied against a common enemy (b) engaged in a war (c) neighboring (d) peace-loving

16. a *flippant* attitude
    (a) jokingly disrespectful (b) cold and distant (c) highly dignified (d) warm and friendly

17. to emerge from the *maze*
    (a) complicated network of passages (b) secret hiding place (c) tunnel that cuts through a hill (d) heavy fog

18. A *blizzard* was forecast.

(a) thunderstorm (b) dry spell (c) rainstorm (d) heavy snowstorm

19. to prevent a *recurrence*
    (a) accident (b) illness (c) argument (d) repetition

20. *murky* water
    (a) clear and sparkling (b) poisoned (c) salt (d) dark and gloomy

21. a sharp *twinge*
    (a) Indian arrow (b) curved Eastern dagger (c) sudden pain (d) curve in a road

22. a *twinge* of guilt
    (a) confession (b) anxious feeling (c) sign (d) assumption

Check your answers against the correct ones below. The answers are not in order; this is to prevent your eye catching sight of the correct ones before you have had a chance to do the exercise on your own.

14b. 3a. 18d. 7c. 4d. 9c. 17a. 21c. 12d. 6a. 8c. 2b. 13c. 16a. 11b. 15b. 1b. 19d. 5b. 22b. 10c. 20d.

Go back to your dictionary and look up again those words for which you gave incorrect answers. Only after doing this should you go on to the next exercise.

EXERCISE 10B

Each word from Word List 10 is used four times in the following sentences; one of the sentences in each group uses the word incorrectly. You are to circle the letter that precedes that sentence. Do not circle more than one letter in any one group.

1. (a) I felt a *twinge* of regret when it came time to leave home. (b) His old wound sometimes *twinges* when the weather gets cold. (c) She felt a *twinge* of envy when her friend won the athletic award. (d) Ivy *twinged* around the old wooden columns in front of the house.

2. (a) They are taking *extensive* precautions to prevent any further accidents. (b) She owns *extensive* lands in South America. (c) An *extensive* boulder lay directly across their path. (d) The hurricane caused *extensive* damage along the coast.

3. (a) She poked her head *timorously* out of the tent to see who was there. (b) The townspeople are a *timorous* lot, afraid to express an opinion which is not accepted. (c) While the battle lasted, the air was *timorous* with the clash of steel and the cries of the wounded. (d) The captain spoke to the men in such a *timorous* voice that they questioned his ability to lead them.

4. (a) His *flippant* attitude annoyed his more serious friends. (b) Her continued *flippancy* in class is disturbing to the other children. (c) We all laughed at the way she *flippanted* across the room. (d) "Don't harm my beard," the condemned man said *flippantly*, just before he was beheaded.

5. (a) Shyness can keep a person in *bondage* more effectively than chains. (b) Moses led the Jewish people out of *bondage* in Egypt. (c) His friend offered to put up $500 *bondage* to keep him out of jail. (d) Abraham Lincoln's Emancipation Proclamation released the slaves from nearly two hundred years of *bondage*.

6. (a) His experiences in the war had *unscathed* his mind. (b) Although bullets flew all around us, we were *unscathed*. (c) The Indian holy man was able to walk *unscathed* over burning coals in his bare feet. (d) Not a single man emerged *unscathed* from the battle.

7. (a) Trash cans are *indisposed* at intervals along the sea front. (b) She is *indisposed* and is spending the day in bed. (c) The bank manager seemed *indisposed* to help me when I told her of my difficulty. (d) She is recovered from her recent *indisposition* and is now receiving visitors.

8. (a) The arctic explorers huddled in their tent and waited for the *blizzard* to blow over.

(b) "I'm the greatest!" the new boxing champion *blizzarded.* (c) A light snowfall in the afternoon had turned into a full *blizzard* by nightfall. (d) The great Boston *blizzard* of 1978 left 29 inches of snow.

9. (a) I was assured there would be no *recurrence* of the problem. (b) A deep *recurrence,* believed caused by an earthquake, cut through the mountain range. (c) If there should be a *recurrence* of the symptoms, see your doctor immediately. (d) They are doing everything possible to prevent a *recurrence* of last month's rioting.

10. (a) Her voice *haltered,* and she stopped reading for a moment and wiped a tear from her eye. (b) She wore a *halter* that was open at the back and fastened around the neck by a loop. (c) The *halter* was placed around the neck of the condemned man, and the trapdoor under his feet was sprung. (d) He slipped a *halter* over the bull's head and led it into the ring.

11. (a) The water lily is one of the most beautiful *aquatic* plants. (b) She bought a large *aquatic* in which to keep her tropical fish. (c) He loves all *aquatic* sports, particularly water polo. (d) Seals, porpoises, and other *aquatic* animals are on display at the zoo.

12. (a) He saw nothing noble in the battlefield, littered with twisted corpses; rather, it seemed somehow *obscene.* (b) She tried to *obscene* her plans in an attempt to throw us off the scent. (c) The Supreme Court has the difficult task of deciding what is *obscene.* (d) The driver kicked the horses and screamed *obscenities* at them, but they refused to move.

13. (a) He had no desire for anyone to probe into his admittedly *murky* past. (b) She grabbed the young *murky* by the arm and questioned him closely. (c) She stared for a moment into the *murky* depths of the pool. (d) All week long the rain poured down from the *murky* skies.

14. (a) Her reply was expressed in such *belligerent*

terms that I chose to ignore it. (b) Germany, Italy, and Japan were co-*belligerents* in World War II. (c) The huge rock was poised *belligerently* above the narrow pass. (d) His *belligerent* attitude sometimes frightens the other boys.

15. (a) He found himself caught up in a *maze* of legal entanglements. (b) She conducts experiments in which rats have to find their way through *mazes.* (c) It was great fun wandering through the *maze* that had been laid out in the grounds of the graden. (d) It will *maze* you when you find out how simple it is.

16. (a) Much of the land in Holland has been *acclaimed* from the sea. (b) The whole world *acclaimed* Lindbergh's feat of flying solo across the Atlantic. (c) The winner was received with loud *acclaim.* (d) Amid much rejoicing, the crown prince was *acclaimed* king.

EXERCISE 10C

Rewrite each of the sentences below, replacing the italicized word or phrase with a word from Word List 10 and writing the word in the form that fits the rest of the sentence. Use each word only once. Write your answers in the spaces provided.

1. The *heavy snowstorm* caused *widespread* damage to the spring crops.

   . . . .

   . . . .

2. She told her doctor she had felt *sudden, sharp pains* once or twice during the night but reported no *repetition* of the pain during the day.

   . . . .

   . . . .

3. The boxer was *greeted with loud applause* by the spectators after regaining the title and

emerging from the fight *without any harm to himself.*

....

....

4. I received a *saucy and disrespectful* answer when I asked the students if they were interested in *water* sports

....

....

5. The king agreed to release the man from *his condition of slavery* if he could find his way out of the *intricate and confusing set of interconnecting passageways* that the king had had built.

....

....

6. After falling into the *dark and dirty* water of the dock, she was *slightly ill* for a few days.

....

....

7. The defendant's *shocking and immoral* language was a further indication of his *quarrelsome and hostile* attitude.

....

....

8. The horse was *easily frightened* and tried to shake off the *rope that was put around its neck and used for leading.*

....

....

EXERCISE 10D

The Latin *aqua,* meaning "water" gives us the word AQUATIC, which means "having to do with water."

Using the root *aqua,* sometimes spelled *aque,* complete the words below for which other roots and suffixes have been supplied. Write out a brief definition of each word. Check each word and definition in your dictionary for accuracy and spelling.

1. _____plane

....

2. _____rium

....

3. _____duct

....

4. _____lung

....

5. _____marine

....

6. _____ cade

....

7. _____ tint

....

8. _____ous

....

EXERCISE 10E

Write out, in the spaces provided, the words from Word List 10 for which a definition, homonym, synonym, or antonym is given on the next page.

When you are asked to give a root or a prefix, you should refer back to the preceding exercise; the information you require will be found there. Make sure that each of your answers has the same number of letters as there are spaces. A definition followed by a number is a review word; the number gives the Word List from which it is taken.

If all the words are filled in correctly, the boxes running up and down the answer spaces will continue the riddle begun earlier.

1. an antonym for *grave*

2. a violent snowstorm

3. a state of confusion

4. an antonym for *willing*

5. having to do with water

6. offensive to modesty or decency

7. a sudden, sharp pain

8. a synonym for *widespread*

9. an antonym for *harmed*

10. a synonym for *warlike*

11. an open insult (3)

12. a synonym for *praise*

13. something that happens again

14. to cause, urge, or influence to do something (6)

15. a rope or strap for leading an animal

16. a synonym for *slavery*

17. a Latin root meaning "water"

18. an antonym for *clear*

19. an antonym for *bold*

20. weak or feeble from sickness or old age (2)

WORDLY WISE 10

Up until 1881, a BLIZZARD was simply a loud noise or blast. In that year, the *New York Nation*, commenting on heavy snowstorms of the previous winter, said: "The hard weather has called into use a word which promises to become a national Americanism, namely *blizzard.* It designates a storm of snow and wind which we cannot resist away from shelter." Thus, the word came to have its present meaning. Officially a *blizzard* is a storm with winds above forty m.p.h., a temperature close to zero, and an abundance of fine snow.

The most famous MAZE in legend is the labyrinth made for King Minos, a ruler of ancient Crete, by the great engineer Daedalus. When it was complete, the king put Daedalus and his son Icarus into the maze and challenged them to find their way out. Daedalus outwitted the king by constructing wings out of feathers held together with wax. He and his son then escaped by flying out of the labyrinth.

Word List 11

CASTIGATE	EFFECTIVE	INURED
COMPLICATED	EXCEPTIONAL	PARABLE
CREATE	EXPLETIVE	PLAUSIBLE
DIRE	FLUCTUATE	SEMBLANCE
DOGGEREL	GNOME	ZEALOUS

Look up the words above in your dictionary. Note that some of the words have more than one meaning. When you feel that you know *all* the meanings of *all* the words, go on to the exercise below.

EXERCISE 11A

From the four choices under each phrase or sentence, you are to mark the one that is closest in meaning to the word appearing in italics. When the same word appears more than once, you should note that it is being used in a different sense.

1. a *plausible* story
   (a) long and rambling (b) obviously untrue (c) apparently true (d) hastily put together

2. to *castigate* a student
   (a) praise (b) explain something to (c) scold severely (d) put out of school

3. a few pages of *doggerel*
   (a) poorly-written prose (b) loosely styled verse (c) instructions (d) amusing drawings

4. She read us a *parable.*
   (a) amusing poem (b) important letter (c) article in a newspaper (d) short story teaching a lesson

5. a *complicated* problem
   (a) not expected (b) not simple (c) not serious (d) not understood

6. *effective* tomorrow
   (a) forgotten (b) in force (c) ready (d) needed

7. It was *effective.*
   (a) used very sparingly (b) held in readiness (c) able to produce the desired result (d) useless for the purpose intended

8. a *zealous* general
   (a) too timid (b) very enthusiastic (c) easily-angered (d) lazy and careless

9. to *create* a masterpiece
   (a) bring into being (b) admire greatly (c) discover (d) long to own

10. a friendly *gnome*
    (a) talking animal (b) fairy-tale dwarf (c) giant (d) gesture

11. a *semblance* of order
    (a) outward appearance (b) complete lack (c) steadily increasing breakdown (d) fine example

12. *dire* misfortune
    (a) slight (b) dreadful (c) unexpected (d) predicted

13. an *exceptional* performance
    (a) dull and boring (b) unusually good (c) solo (d) single

14. loud *expletives*
    (a) demands (b) cries for help (c) explosions (d) swearwords

15. *Expletives* fill out the line.
    (a) words without meaning in the sentence (b) words beginning with the same letter (c) words that appeal to the emotions (d) out-of-date words

16. *inured* to criticism
    (a) subjected (b) accustomed (c) sensitive (d) exposed

17. The prices *fluctuate*.
    (a) go up and down (b) rise constantly (c) remain unchanged (d) are deliberately kept high

Check your answers against the correct ones below. The answers are not in order; this is to prevent your eye catching sight of the correct ones before you have had a chance to do the exercise on your own.

14d. 3b. 7c. 4d. 9a. 10b. 12b. 6b. 8b. 2c. 13b. 16b. 11a. 15a. 1c. 5b. 17a.

Go back to your dictionary and look up again those words for which you gave incorrect answers. Only after doing this should you go on to the next exercise.

EXERCISE 11B

Each word from Word List 11 is used four times in the following sentences; one of the sentences in each group uses the word incorrectly. You are to circle the letter that precedes that sentence. Do not circle more than one letter in any one group.

1. (a) Life today is much more *complicated* than it was a hundred years ago. (b) The puzzle was more *complicated* than it had looked at first. (c) The oats were *complicated* with hay and fed to the horses. (d) The problem of where everyone would sleep was *complicated* by the unexpected arrival of more guests.

2. (a) *Dire* misfortune awaited the explorers who broke into the tomb of the ancient Egyptian king. (b) Don't let him *dire* you into doing something you don't want to do. (c) Only persons in *dire* need should apply for help. (d) She uttered *dire* threats as to what would happen to us.

3. (a) *Expletives* fill out the line without adding to the meaning. (b) In the sentence "Make it clear why you dislike her," "it" is an *expletive*. (c) The situation was *expletive* for a few moments until everyone calmed down. (d) His speech was filled with mild *expletives* like "Gosh!" and "Darn!"

4. (a) We went fishing for *doggerel* off the end of the pier. (b) She wrote occasional pieces of *doggerel* which her friends were kind enough to call poetry. (c) *Doggerel* verse can be amusing provided one does not take it seriously. (d) There were a few good lines in the poem, but most of it was pure *doggerel*.

5. (a) Many religious teachings are expressed in *parables*. (b) The children in the class were asked what they thought the *parable* meant. (c) The *parable* of the prodigal son tells of the return of an erring son to his loving father. (d) He drew a curve on the paper in the shape of a *parable*.

6. (a) I thought your *castigation* of the two girls was too severe. (b) The poem *castigates* humanity for its failure to put an end to war. (c) It was unnecessary for him to *castigate* his people for their actions. (d) We put soothing ointment on her *castigations* to take away the pain.

7. (a) She *fluctuated* her words carefully so that all might hear. (b) The price of wheat *fluctuated* wildly because of uncertainties about the harvest. (c) The temperature *fluctuations* are recorded on these instruments (d) Her mood *fluctuated* between black despair and pure joy.

8. (a) Her story was very *plausibly* told; however I didn't believe it. (b) He's a *plausible* rogue, and you'd be well advised to have nothing to do

do with him. (c) Fish were so *plausible* in the lake that we caught ten in a couple of minutes. (d) Her story sounds *implausible,* but could be true.

9. (a) Everyone must attend, and there are to be no *exceptionals.* (b) She is an *exceptional* child and should do well in whatever she attempts. (c) There have been an *exceptional* number of rainy days this summer. (d) This has been an *exceptionally* trying time for all of us.

10. (a) They were *inured* to the cold and thought it quite mild when the temperature was zero. (b) The public is *inured* to the promises of the politicians. (c) The wet cement is poured into molds and left until it has *inured.* (d) Forty years in politics had *inured* him to criticism.

11. (a) She *zealously* defended the right of any state to withdraw from the Union. (b) His story was obviously *zealous,* but he refused to admit he was lying. (c) He was a *zealous* worker, who lived only for his art. (d) The police were *zealous* in their pursuit of the lawbreakers.

12. (a) Aspirin is the most *effective* remedy for a headache. (b) She would be a more *effective* speaker if she sounded surer of her facts. (c) The bill passed by Congress becomes *effective* as soon as the president signs it. (d) A glass of lemon juice makes a good *effective* against colds.

13. (a) He did his best to maintain a *semblance* of neatness, but it was a hopeless task. (b) She tried to throw a *semblance* over the facts, but no one was deceived. (c) The agreement had the *semblance* of a pact between equals, but actually it was far from this. (d) Her story possesses not even a *semblance* of the truth.

14 (a) The *gnome* "Art is long, and life is short" is one of my favorite expressions. (b) They had a number of plaster *gnomes* arranged in their garden. (c) His short legs and stocky body gave him a *gnomish* appearance. (d) Her face was *gnomed* and wrinkled with age.

15. (a) The teacher wants to know who *created* the disturbance. (b) The orange *create* can be broken up for firewood. (c) It was once believed that the world was created in 4004 B.C. (d) The pope *created* three new cardinals yesterday.

EXERCISE 11C
Rewrite each of the sentences below, replacing the italicized word or phrase with a word from Word List 11 and writing the word in the form that fits the rest of the sentence. Use each word only once. Write your answers in the spaces provided.

1. The factors that cause prices to *keep rising and falling* are very *complex and involved.*

. . . .

. . . .

2. He thought that sprinkling his speech with *oaths and swearwords* would make it more *likely to achieve the desired result.*

. . . .

. . . .

3. His fellow poets accused him of writing *very bad verse,* but he was *accustomed* to such criticism.

. . . .

. . . .

4. The *little bearded dwarf in the fairy tale* guarded the treasure *very enthusiastically* because *dreadful* misfortune would follow if it were stolen.

. . . .

. . . .

5. Generally, his stories seem *as though they might be true,* but this one has not even the

outward appearance of truth.

. . . .

. . . .

6. The teacher *spoke scoldingly to* the children for not paying attention while he was reading the *short story teaching a lesson.*

. . . .

. . . .

7. I have an *unusually good* opportunity to buy a sculpture that the artist *produced* just before she died.

. . . .

. . . .

EXERCISE 11D

A very common Latin prefix is *ex-*, which means "out" or "from." It is found in such words as EXPLETIVE, "a word or phrase used to fill *out* a line or a sentence," and in EXCEPTIONAL, which literally means "taken *out,*" and hence "different" or "unusual." For ease in pronunciation, *ex-* is written *e-* before the following letters: *b, d, g, l, m, n, r,* and *v.*

Complete the words below by adding the appropriate form of the prefix *ex-* or *e-*. Write out a brief definition of each word, checking in your dictionary for correctness of spelling and accuracy of meaning.

1. __rase

. . . .

2. __claim

. . . .

3. __mit

. . . .

4. __hale

. . . .

5. __pel

. . . .

You should know that in addition to meaning "out," the Latin prefix *ex-* or *e-* may also mean "beyond" (as in *excess*), "upward" (as in *extol*), "greatly" (as in *exhilarating*), and "former" (as in *ex-husband*).

After each of the words below, write out in the parentheses the meaning of the italicized prefix. Write out a brief definition of each word, checking in your dictionary for correctness of spelling and accuracy of meaning.

6. *ex*-convict (   )

. . . .

7. *ex*ceed (   )

. . . .

8. *ex*ult (   )

. . . .

9. *ex*clude (   )

. . . .

10. *ex*alt (   )

. . . .

EXERCISE 11E

Write out, in the spaces provided, the words from Word List 11 for which a definition, homonym, synonym, or antonym is given on the next page. When you are asked to give a root or a prefix, you should refer back to the preceding exercise; the information you require will be found there. Make sure that each of your answers has the same number of letters as there are spaces. A definition followed by a number is a review word; the number gives the Word List from which it is taken.

If all the words are filled in correctly, the boxes running up and down the answer spaces will continue the riddle begun earlier.

1. to scold severely

2. an antonym for *ordinary*

3. a synonym for *dreadful*

4. an antonym for *simple*

5. an oath or exclamation

?

6. a synonym for *likeness*

7. a Latin prefix meaning "out"

8. an antonym for *useless*

9. a short story that contains a moral

10. a synonym for *believable*

11. extremely enthusiastic

12. a synonym for *accustomed*

13. a synonym for *vary*

14. to fascinate (7)

15. verse loosely constructed for comic effect

16. a very deep crack in the earth's surface (4)

17. unharmed (10)

18. to bring into being

19. open; not hidden or secret (6)

20. a bearded dwarf in fairy tales

GNOME is one of those words where the "g" is silent; pronounce this word *nome*. The word is derived from a legendary species of small beings, usually described as shriveled little old men, who inhabit the interior of the earth and act as guardians of its treasures. *Gnome* has another less common meaning: "a short, concise expression of a general truth." This meaning stems from the Greek word for "judgment" or "opinion."

A *resemblance* is a similarity or likeness, as in the sentence, "She bears a strong *resemblance* to her mother." SEMBLANCE suggests a *seeming* likeness, an outward appearance or show, as in this sentence, "He made an effort to give his business a *semblance* of success."

Zeal is pronounced *zeel*; however, its adjectival form, ZEALOUS, is pronounced *ZEL-us*.

Word List 12

ALLUDE	DISRUPT	PARE
AUTHENTIC	ELIMINATE	RAMPANT
BATON	HIRELING	SCOURGE
CLARITY	KNELL	TRIPLICATE
COCKADE	LEI	UNSEEMLY

Look up the words above in your dictionary. Note that some of the words have more than one meaning. When you feel that you know *all* the meanings of *all* the words, go on to the exercise below.

EXERCISE 12A

From the four choices under each phrase or sentence, you are to mark the one that is closest in meaning to the word appearing in italics. When the same word appears more than once, you should note that it is being used in a different sense.

1. to *pare* an apple
   (a) peel (b) cut up (c) eat (d) pick

2. to *pare* the cost
   (a) be unable to afford (b) estimate roughly (c) cut down on (d) keep a record

3. a blue *cockade*
   (a) band worn around the arm (b) ribbon worn on a hat (c) bird that resembles a jay (d) sash worn across the chest

4. She accepted the *lei*.
   (a) ring of flowers worn around the neck (b) skirt made of long strands of grass (c) wrap-around cotton skirt (d) necklace of shark's teeth

5. to *disrupt* the class

   (a) attend (b) disturb (c) enroll in (d) withdraw from

6. to *allude* to the next case
   (a) refer (b) proceed (c) be assigned (d) object

7. to *scourge* someone
   (a) whip (b) reward (c) scrub (d) follow closely behind

8. This war is a *scourge*.
   (a) means of acquiring new lands (b) necessary evil (c) result of a misunderstanding (d) cause of terrible suffering

9. She raised the *baton*.
   (a) whip used on horses (b) single-shot rifle (c) sights on a rifle (d) stick used to conduct an orchestra

10. He practices with a *baton*.
    (a) small piano-like instrument (b) partner in certain field sports (c) teacher of music (d) metal rod that is twirled showily

11. to *eliminate* a danger
    (a) be aware of (b) be the cause of (c) remove (d) ignore

12. *unseemly* language
    (a) dignified (b) improper (c) obscure (d) flowery

13. with great *clarity*
    (a) clearness (b) interest (c) anger (d) joy

14. the funeral *knell*
    (a) service conducted at the grave (b) party

given after the service (c) slow tolling of bells (d) procession from the church

15. Everything is done in *triplicate*.
    (a) two copies (b) three copies (c) four copies (d) five copies

16. The signature is *authentic*.
    (a) boldly written (b) unclear (c) genuine (d) false

17. He is merely a *hireling*.
    (a) person who refuses to get involved (b) person in the pay of another (c) person blamed for another's crime (d) person forced by others to do wrong

18. The disease was *rampant*.
    (a) spreading wildly (b) deadly (c) under control (d) greatly feared

Check your answers against the correct ones below. The answers are not in order; this is to prevent your eye catching sight of the correct ones before you have had a chance to do the exercise on your own.

14c. 3b. 18a. 7a. 4a. 9d. 17b. 12b. 6a. 8d. 2c. 13a. 16c. 11c. 15b. 1a. 5b. 10d.

Go back to your dictionary and look up again those words for which you gave incorrect answers. Only after doing this should you go on to the next exercise.

EXERCISE 12B

Each word from Word List 12 is used four times in the following sentences; one of the sentences in each group uses the word incorrectly. You are to circle the letter that precedes that sentence. Do not circle more than one letter in any one group.

1. (a) He attached the *cockade* to his hat and stepped outside. (b) *Cockaded* guards parade in front of the palace gates. (c) *Cockades* strutted about the farmyard, their feathers ruffling in the wind. (d) The men wore hats decorated with blue and white *cockades*.

2. (a) The islanders swayed in time to the soft music of the *lei*. (b) They make *leis* out of flowers, leaves, shells, or whatever else is available. (c) Each child was given a party hat and a brightly-colored paper *lei*. (d) The islanders wore *leis* made of twisted flowers around their necks.

3. (a) Mark Twain's *authentic* name was Samuel Langhorne Clemens. (b) This letter, signed by Dolly Madison, is undoubtedly *authentic*. (c) This book gives an *authentic* account of life in the Middle Ages. (d) This painting has been *authenticated* as a genuine Rembrandt.

4. (a) It is *unseemly* to discuss such subjects in front of the children. (b) His health has been *unseemly* lately, and he is confined to his bed. (c) Bells rang at the most *unseemly* hours, day and night. (d) An *unseemly* quarrel had broken out which threatened to divide the family.

5. (a) She has been feeling a little below *pare* lately. (b) The prime minister said she has *pared* the budget considerably by reducing military expenditures. (c) Use a sharp knife to *pare* the potatoes. (d) Don't let the *parings* from your fingernails fall on the floor.

6. (a) She refused the job because the amount of traveling would *disrupt* her family life. (b) She kept trying to *disrupt* him while he was speaking. (c) A few rowdies got in and tried to *disrupt* the meeting. (d) Traffic on the highway was *disrupted* by a five-car collision.

7. (a) She was amazed at the *clarity* of the atmosphere in the mountains. (b) The liquid was cloudy at first but soon recovered its *clarity*. (c) The *clarity* and forcefulness of her speech impressed everyone. (d) You can *clarity* the liquid by passing it through a filter.

8. (a) Rumor ran *rampant* in those first few days. (b) Smallpox was *rampant* in the area, and many people died. (c) A *rampant* of earth and boulders protected the fort from attack. (d) In a coat of arms, a lion *rampant* is one pictured

rearing up with one foreleg raised above the other.

9. (a) He pretended to know nothing of the crime committed by his *hirelings*. (b) She lets her *hirelings* do her dirty work. (c) The company has five thousand *hirelings* working at its main plant in Chicago. (d) The young princess was murdered by *hirelings* of her uncle.

10. (a) Which cheerleader won the *baton*-twirling contest? (b) The field marshal carried a *baton* as a symbol of his rank. (c) The sailors rushed to *baton* down the hatches when the storm came up. (d) The conductor silenced the orchestra by tapping sharply with his *baton*.

11. (a) We listened in silence to the mournful *knell* of the church bells. (b) All day the *knell* rang out its mournful sound. (c) The invention of the automobile sounded the *knell* of the horse and buggy. (d) With heavy hearts, we listened to the bells *knell* the passing of our beloved president.

12. (a) The answer to the problem continues to *allude* me. (b) What was the incident to which she kept *alluding*? (c) She *alluded* to large sums of money hidden about the place. (d) The poet *alludes* frequently to her experiences in early youth.

13. (a) They *scourged* the countryside in a vain search for the missing children. (b) The guards *scourged* the prisoner before throwing him into the dungeon. (c) She looked forward to a world free of the *scourge* of war. (d) Diphtheria, once a terrible childhood *scourge*, has practically been wiped out.

14. (a) The kidneys and the skin are two parts of the body which help to *eliminate* waste products. (b) Dictators have a habit of *eliminating* anyone who stands in their way. (c) The children soon *eliminated* their money and came back for more. (d) *Eliminate* everything that is not essential.

15. (a) She used *triplicate* forms so that each of the three partners would have a copy. (b) Keep the first two copies and give the *triplicate* to the customer. (c) The mother was overjoyed when she gave birth to *triplicates*. (d) All forms must be completed in *triplicate*.

EXERCISE 12C

Rewrite each of the sentences below, replacing the italicized word or phrase with a word from Word List 12 and writing the word in the form that fits the rest of the sentence. Use each word only once. Write your answers in the spaces provided.

1. You can tell that this violin is a *genuine* Stradivarius by the *clear quality* of the tone.

. . . .

. . . .

2. I believe it was a *person in the pay* of one of the ranchers who poisoned the water hole.

. . . .

. . . .

3. We must make up our minds to *do away with* the *terrible pain and suffering* of war.

. . . .

. . . .

4. Each form must be completed in *three identical copies.*

. . . .

. . . .

5. The French general wore a *knot of colored ribbon* on his hat and carried a *short stick as a symbol of his rank.*

. . . .

. . . .

6. Upon arriving in Hawaii, we were each given a *narrow wreath of flowers* to wear around our necks.

. . . .

. . . .

7. It was *most improper* of you to *make a reference* to his criminal past.

. . . .

. . . .

8. Strikes are *completely out of control* in the country and threaten to *break up* the entire economy of the nation.

. . . .

. . . .

9. Mother asked me to *trim away the skin from* the apples.

. . . .

. . . .

10. The *slow, solemn tolling* of the church bells marked the death of the president.

. . . .

. . . .

EXERCISE 12D

TRIPLICATE, meaning "made in three copies," comes from the Latin word *tri*, which means "three." A large number of our words come from Latin or Greek numbers, and it will be useful to review them here. The most common are those in the table below.

	Latin	Greek
1	uni-	mono-
2	duo-, bi-	di-
3	tri-	tri-
4	quad-	tetra-
5	quin-	penta-
6	sex-	hexa-
7	sept-	hepta-
8	octo-	octa-
9	non-, nov-	ennea-
10	decem-	deca-
100	centi-	hecto-, heca-
1000	milli-	kilo-

In addition, you should know that "half" is *semi-* in Latin and *hemi-* or *demi-* in Greek.

Complete the sentences below.

1. A hectogram is a weight of . . . . grams.

2. Biweekly payments are made every . . . . weeks.

3. September was the . . . . month of the Roman calendar.

4. A hemisphere is . . . .

5. Quadruplets are . . . . babies born to a mother at one time.

6. A demigod is a creature that is . . . .

7. A decade is a period of . . . . years.

8. A millipede is supposed to have . . . . legs.

9. An octagon is a figure that has . . . . sides.

10. A semiannual event is held . . . .

11. A novena is a Catholic act of worship that lasts . . . . days.

12. A centurion was a Roman officer commanding . . . . men.

13. A kilometer is a distance of . . . . meters.

14. A pentagram is a . . . . pointed star.

15. A sextet is a group of . . . . singers or performers.

EXERCISE 12E

Write out, in the spaces provided, the words from Word List 12 for which a definition, homonym, synonym, or antonym is given below. When you are asked to give a root or a prefix, you should refer back to the preceding exercise; the information you require will be found there. Make sure that each of your answers has the same number of letters as there are spaces. A definition followed by a number is a review word; the number gives the Word List from which it is taken.

If all the words are filled in correctly, the boxes running up and down the answer spaces will continue the riddle begun earlier.

1. to make reference to

2. an antonym for *proper*

3. a synonym for *clearness*

4. a Latin or Greek prefix meaning "three"

5. a person in the pay of another

6. a synonym for *uncontrolled*

7. made in three copies

8. an antonym for *fake*

9. to cut or trim away the rind or skin

10. a colored ribbon worn on a hat

11. a stick used by an orchestra conductor

12. long-lasting (7)

13. the slow, mournful tolling of a bell

14. a garland of flowers worn around the neck

15. a synonym for *remove*

16. to spoil the orderliness of; to break up

17. something that causes great and widespread suffering

18. to hold back from doing (9)

WORDLY WISE 12

Elude means "to escape or get away from." ALLUDE means to "to refer to indirectly or in a general way." Don't confuse these two words.

KNELL, pronounced *nel,* may be a verb or a noun; when it is used as a noun, it means (1) the sound of a bell slowly rung, as at a funeral, (2) a warning that something will, or has, ended or passed away. The word does not refer to the actual bell itself.

Two notes on pronunciation: SCOURGE is pronounced *skurj;* LEI is pronounced *lay.*

ACROSS

2. a knot of ribbon worn on a hat
9. to refer to
13. growing wildly
14. believable; possible
15. easily frightened
16. hostile; warlike
17. a large mass of floating ice (3)
20. a sharp pain
21. weak; feeble (2)
23. a narrow stick
24. to bring into being
26. dark and gloomy
27. widespread
28. unwilling
34. beaming (3)
35. enthusiastic
37. disrespectful in a joking manner
39. a person in the pay of another
40. repetition
41. accustomed
44. a confusing network of passages
45. to do away with
46. slavery
47. likeness; similarity
48. to waver; vary

DOWN

1. a short story with a moral
2. not simple; complex
3. clearness
4. real; genuine
5. an exclamation
6. made in three copies
7. a rope for leading an animal
8. to scold sharply
10. a circle of flowers worn around the neck
11. desperately urgent; dismal
12. not proper; unbecoming
18. a fairy-tale dwarf
19. to disturb
22. unharmed
23. a heavy snowstorm
25. outstanding
29. something that causes great pain or suffering
30. immoral; indecent
31. bringing about the desired results
32. the slow ringing of a bell
33. loosely styled, comic verse
36. to greet loudly
38. of the water
42. a stupid person (1)
43. to peel off the skin or rind

Chapter Five

Word List 13

ABSTAIN	EXPOSE	PASSAGE
AGGRAVATE	FATEFUL	PREMONITION
AVALANCHE	FUME	SHREW
COLLABORATE	IMPASSE	TOADY
CREDITOR	MITE	UNEARTHLY
EXAGGERATE		

Look up the words above in your dictionary. Note that some of the words have more than one meaning. When you feel that you know *all* the meanings of *all* the words, go on to the exercise below.

EXERCISE 13A

From the four choices under each phrase or sentence, you are to mark the one that is closest in meaning to the word appearing in italics. When the same word appears more than once, you should note that it is being used in a different sense.

1. a detestable *toady*
   (a) liar (b) beggar (c) flatterer (d) criminal

2. a narrow *passage*
   (a) bridge wide enough for one person (b) place for people to pass (c) escape (d) one-way street

3. an uneventful *passage*
   (a) evening (b) period of time (c) vacation (d) crossing by boat

4. Change the last *passage*.
   (a) item (b) part of a design (c) part of something written (d) name

5. to escape the *avalanche*
   (a) violent trembling of the earth (b) mass of snow sliding down a mountain (c) forest fire caused by a dry spell (d) overflowing of the banks of a river

6. an *avalanche* of mail
   (a) large canvas sack (b) decrease in volume (c) trickle (d) sudden large volume

7. a sudden *premonition*
   (a) feeling that something bad will happen (b) sharp pain (c) calm before a violent storm (d) attack from all sides at once

8. *fumes* from the fire
   (a) smoke (b) ashes (c) flames (d) sparks

9. She *fumed* when told to wait.
   (a) showed great irritation (b) smiled resignedly (c) remained calm (d) left hurriedly

10. a friendly *creditor*
    (a) person who sells below cost (b) judge in a small debts court (c) person to whom one owes money (d) person who owes money

11. *unearthly* sounds
    (a) that cannot be heard (b) weird (c) underground (d) constantly changing

12. to *aggravate* the illness
    (a) recover from (b) make worse (c) be exposed to (d) discover a cure for

13. to reach an *impasse*
    (a) decision agreeable to all (b) opening in a mountain range (c) solution to a problem (d) difficulty that cannot be resolved

14. a tiny *shrew*
    (a) evergreen shrub (b) cricketlike insect (c) bird with a long, thin, beak (d) mouselike animal

15. a *shrewish* woman
    (a) tiny (b) clever (c) nagging (d) lazy

16. a *fateful* decision
    (a) sudden (b) jointly arrived at (c) very important (d) unpopular

17. *fateful* words
    (a) telling of the future (b) spoken in anger (c) spoken in sorrow (d) harsh-sounding

18. a *fateful* error
(a) deliberate (b) trifling (c) deadly (d) foolish

19. to *abstain from* strong drink
(a) weaken by adding water (b) have a fondness for (c) make for one's own use (d) do without willingly

20. How many *abstained*?
(a) did not attend the meeting (b) remained behind (c) voted in the election (d) refused to vote for or against

21. the widow's *mite*
(a) black shawl (b) poorly-furnished house (c) little store of food (d) small sum of money

22. to study the *mite*
(a) sea creature like the octopus (b) very detailed design (c) plant that grows on rocks (d) small animal of the spider family

23. to *collaborate* on a book
(a) write a report (b) put hard covers (c) work together (d) make a secret mark

24. Its size was *exaggerated*.
(a) constantly changing (b) well known to everyone (c) made to seem greater than it was (d) not yet determined

25. an *exposed* position
(a) secluded (b) enviable (c) unprotected (d) comfortable

26. to *expose* the plans
(a) work carefully on (b) make known (c) cover up (d) copy in great detail

27. to *expose* the film
(a) load into a camera (b) show on a screen (c) let light fall on (d) bring out the picture on

28. an exciting *exposé*
(a) journey in a foreign land (b) high point of a film or play (c) revealing of unsavory facts (d) dream remembered in every detail

Check your answers against the correct ones below. The answers are not in order; this is to prevent your eye catching sight of the correct ones before you have had a chance to do the exercise on your own.

3d. 14d. 24c. 18c. 7a. 20d. 4c. 23c. 9a. 17a. 26b. 21d. 12b. 6d. 8a. 25c. 2b. 13d. 16c. 28c. 11b. 15c. 27c. 1c. 19d. 5b. 22d. 10c.

Go back to your dictionary and look up again those words for which you gave incorrect answers. Only after doing this should you go on to the next exercise.

EXERCISE 13B

Each word from Word List 13 is used four times in the sentences below; one of the sentences in each group uses the word incorrectly. You are to circle the letter that precedes that sentence. Do not circle more than one letter in any one group.

1. (a) "Reports of my death have been greatly *exaggerated*," said Mark Twain, wittily. (b) She has an *exaggerated* idea of her own importance. (c) We will have to *exaggerate* the cupboard to make more room. (d) He *exaggerated* his illness in order to get more sympathy.

2. (a) She is surrounded by *toadies*, who tell her exactly what she wants to hear. (b) He is a *toady* fellow, very agreeable to those who can help him. (c) She *toadies* to those in power in a shameful fashion. (d) The small-time politicians and their *toadies* scramble for the rewards of office.

3. (a) Discussions have reached an *impasse* and have been broken off. (b) By backing both parties, he has placed himself in an *impasse*. (c) It is impossible to *impasse* the mountain roads in the winter. (d) The *impasse* was broken when the other side agreed to our terms.

4. (a) I *exposed* that we leave, but the others preferred to stay. (b) If copper is *exposed* to the

73

weather, it turns green. (c) The detective waited until the last moment before *exposing* the murderer. (d) By visiting their cousin, the children were *exposed* to the measles.

5. (a) An *unearthly* green light came from the object. (b) She told us frightening tales of imps and goblins and other *unearthly* creatures. (c) The rocket ship became *unearthly* sixty seconds after lift-off. (d) The *unearthly* cries from the darkness made our blood run cold.

6. (a) Catholics are no longer required to *abstain* from eating meat on Fridays. (b) I *abstained* this table for you. (c) I was neither for nor against the resolution, so I *abstained* when the vote was taken. (d) I *abstained* from saying what I really thought.

7. (a) His *creditors* are pressing him very strongly for their money. (b) She will *creditor* the money to you, if you promise to repay her. (c) She has promised to begin paying back her *creditors* next month. (d) For every *creditor* there is a debtor.

8. (a) It was *shrew* of her to buy up that land so cheaply. (b) Shakespeare's play **The Taming of the** *Shrew* tells how Petruchio tamed his wife, Katherine. (c) Our cat brought home a *shrew* she had killed in the field. (d) Her *shrewish* ways made everyone around her miserable.

9. (a) The strap pressing against his side had *aggravated* his wound. (b) Roads are made by pouring cement on top of *aggravate* and sand. (c) The problems of our cities are *aggravated* by neglect and indifference. (d) The sympathy of her friends served only to *aggravate* her grief.

10. (a) She suffered *fateful* injuries when her car struck a lamppost. (b) The dropping of the atomic bomb on Hiroshima was one of the most *fateful* events of the century. (c) The *fateful* decision to launch the attack had already been made. (d) He remembered vividly the *fateful* words of the old gypsy woman.

11. (a) The falling leaves were a *premonition* of the coming of winter. (b) She gave a mild *premonition* to the children for talking in class. (c) She had a sudden *premonition* of evil when she saw the dark form standing there. (d) "It is a *premonition* of what awaits us," he said when he saw the vultures circling overhead.

12. (a) Exhaust *fumes* from the cars greatly pollute the air. (b) He flew into a *fume* when told to come back later. (c) The whisky *fumes* on his breath were overpowering. (d) She *fumed* at being asked to stand in line behind the others.

13. (a) She had *collaborated* all her friends together to help her. (b) Attempts of the Western countries to *collaborate* with Russia are not always successful. (c) He was found guilty of *collaborating* with the enemy and was executed. (d) Mary Lamb and her brother Charles *collaborated* in writing **Tales from Shakespeare**.

14. (a) The *mites* are too small to be seen, but they burrow under the skin and cause itching. (b) She struggled with *mite* and main to free herself. (c) She is a *mite* less sure of herself than she once was. (d) "A certain poor widow threw in two *mites*."—Mark 2:42

15. (a) An appeal has been *avalanched* to raise funds. (b) An *avalanche* of mail was received by the broadcasting station. (c) A rifle shot in the mountains is enough to trigger an *avalanche*. (d) Many alpine villages live in constant fear of *avalanches*.

16. (a) Each prisoner received a piece of bread and a *passage* of watery soup. (b) He worked his *passage* on a ship to South Africa. (c) Someone bumped into me in the *passage*. (d) Somone has heavily underlined the next *passage*.

EXERCISE 13C

Rewrite each of the following sentences, replacing the italicized word or phrase with a word from Word List 13 and writing the word in the form that fits the rest of the sentence. Use each word only once. Write your answers in the spaces provided.

1. We gave up our attempt to *work together* on the project when we reached a *difficulty that we could not overcome.*

. . . .

. . . .

2. He spoke of those *terribly important* days when victory hung in the balance.

. . . .

. . . .

3. I had an *uneasy feeling* that most of the members would *fail to vote either for or against* when the question was put to the vote.

. . . .

. . . .

4. I do not *make it out to be greater than it actually was* when I say that the roar of the *mass of snow and rock sliding down the mountainside* could be heard ten miles away.

. . . .

. . . .

5. He *showed great anger* when the newspaper threatened to *make known* his criminal activities.

. . . .

. . . .

6. There is a *piece of writing* in the Bible in which the widow's *small sum of money* is said

to be greater than the large offering of a rich man.

. . . .

. . . .

7. *Persons to whom one owes money* are best avoided.

. . . .

. . . .

8. She was a *mean, nagging woman* who did everything she could to *worsen* the situation.

. . . .

. . . .

9. He is an *insincere person who flatters others in order to gain his own ends,* and praise from him means nothing.

. . . .

. . . .

10. The screams from the jungle at night were *so weird that they seemed to be not of this earth,* and they frightened us half to death.

. . . .

. . . .

EXERCISE 13D

A PREMONITION is a feeling that something unpleasant is about to happen; it is a kind of warning. The meaning of this word becomes clear when we see that it is made up of a Latin prefix *pre-,* which means "before," and a Latin root *moni,* which means "to warn."

Complete each of the words below by adding the prefix *pre-.* Write out a brief definition of each word, checking in your dictionary for correctness of spelling and accuracy of meaning.

1. ___CAUTION

· ·

2. ___VIOUS

· ·

3. ___CURSOR

· ·

4. ___CEDE

· ·

5. ___MATURE

· ·

6. ___FIX

· ·

7. ___DICT

· ·

8. ___DECESSOR

· ·

EXERCISE 13E

Write out, in the spaces provided, the words from Word List 13 for which a definition, homonym, synonym, or antonym is given below. When you are asked to give a root or a prefix, you should refer back to the preceding exercise; the information you require will be found there. Make sure that each of your answers has the same number of letters as there are spaces. A definition followed by a number is a review word; the number gives the Word List from which it is taken.

If all the words are filled in correctly, the boxes running up and down the answer spaces will conclude the riddle begun earlier.

1. a situation which cannot be resolved

2. having most important results

3. a synonym for *weird*

4. a very small sum of money

5. a synonym for *worsen*

6. an antonym for *indulge*

7. dark and gloomy; unclear (10)

76

8. a synonym for *reveal*

9. a feeling that something unpleasant
   is about to happen
10. to make something seem greater than it really is

11. an antonym for *debtor*

12. to work together on a project

13. one who flatters others for his own ends

14. to show great anger or irritation

15. a part of a speech or piece of writing

16. a Latin prefix meaning "before"

17. a mass of snow and rocks sliding down a
    mountain
18. a scolding, nagging woman

WORDLY WISE 13

AGGRAVATE, in addition to its correct meaning, is used by some people to mean "annoy." This use, however, is avoided by those who are careful about how they use the English language.

The French word for AVALANCHE is the same as ours—*l'avalanche*. It was influenced by two other French words *à val*, meaning "downhill," or more literally "to the valley," and *avaler,* meaning "to descend."

EXPOSE, as a verb, is pronounced *ik-SPOZE*; when it is a noun meaning "revealing of unsavory facts," it is spelled *expose* or *exposé* and pronounced *EK-spo-ZAY*. The spelling and pronunciation indicate that the word has been brought into the language from French.

FATEFUL and *fatal* overlap slightly in their meanings; however, they are quite different words. *Fatal* is applied to that which leads to death or destruction; *fateful* applies to that which leads to great consequences, good or bad.

Hundreds of years ago, when medicine was far from being the exact science it is today, it was firmly believed that toads were poisonous. Quack doctors had assistants whose job it was to eat, or pretend to eat, toads. The doctor would then proceed to "cure" his assistant, thus proving what a fine medical man he was. The toad-eater naturally had to be somewhat of a flatterer, and a person who flattered others insincerely for his own gain came to be called a *toad-eater;* later, this term was shortened to our modern word TOADY.

Word List 14

ANTHOLOGY	EMBOSS	HANDICAP
ASCERTAIN	EQUESTRIAN	OCTET
ASTUTE	ESPIONAGE	PREOCCUPIED
AURAL	FORBEARANCE	RIFT
CRUCIAL		SUBJUGATE

Look up the words above in your dictionary. Note that some of the words have more than one meaning. When you feel that you know *all* the meanings of *all* the words, go on to the exercise below.

EXERCISE 14A

From the four choices under each phrase or sentence, you are to mark the one that is closest in meaning to the word appearing in italics. When the same word appears more than once, you should note that it is being used in a different sense.

1. to *ascertain* the cost
   (a) object to (b) find out (c) underestimate (d) overestimate

2. to *subjugate* the mob
   (a) join (b) fight with (c) bring under control (d) be fearful of

3. a well-organized *anthology*
   (a) list of books on a subject (b) display of pictures and sculpture (c) collection of poems or stories (d) arrangement of songs

4. a *crucial* test
   (a) long-awaited (b) vitally important (c) surprise (d) carefully prepared for

5. engaged in *espionage*
   (a) spying (b) fighting (c) stealing (d) arguing

6. a serious *handicap*
   (a) disadvantage (b) fault (c) error (d) misunderstanding

7. entered in a *handicap*
   (a) contest in which one has a partner (b) contest made harder for the better participants (c) contest in which the players are disabled

(d) contest in which there is only one winner

8. She sings in an *octet*.
   (a) group of three (b) group of four (c) group of eight (d) group of nine

9. *embossed* wallpaper
   (a) plain (b) vividly-colored (c) with a raised pattern (d) unlike any other

10. an *aural* examination
    (a) of the ears (b) of the eyes (c) of the mouth and throat (d) of the teeth

11. to show *forbearance*
    (a) a willingness to help (b) patience and restraint (c) interest in the affairs of others (d) anger and disgust

12. She seemed *preoccupied*.
    (a) fearful of the future (b) completely absorbed in her thoughts (c) nervous and ill at ease (d) scatterbrained

13. an *astute* person
    (a) amusing (b) foolish (c) clever (d) dull

14. *equestrian* events
    (a) regular (b) horse-riding (c) recorded (d) long ago

15. a *rift* in the earth's surface
    (a) hole (b) crack (c) layer of rock (d) weakness

Check your answers against the correct ones below. The answers are not in order; this is to prevent your eye catching sight of the correct ones before you have had a chance to do the exercise on your own.

14b. 3c. 7b. 4b. 9c. 12b. 6a. 8c. 2c. 13c. 11b. 15b. 1b. 5a. 10a.

Go back to your dictionary and look up again those words for which you gave incorrect answers. Only after doing this should you go on to the next exercise.

78

Each word from Word List 14 is used four times in the sentences below; one of the sentences in each group uses the word incorrectly. You are to circle the letter that precedes that sentence. Do not circle more than one letter in any one group.

1. (a) The eight boys formed an *octet* to play in the school concerts. (b) The musical piece has been arranged as an *octet* and will be played this evening. (c) A sonnet has fourteen lines, the first eight being the *octet* and the last six the sestet. (d) An *octet* is an eight-sided figure.

2. (a) They will *emboss* your initials on the case at no extra charge. (b) Her words will remain forever *embossed* in my memory. (c) My stationery is *embossed* with my family's coat of arms. (d) Lincoln's head is *embossed* on the one-cent piece.

3. (a) The new musical offers *aural* appeal as well as eye-filling spectacle. (b) The medicine is to be taken *aurally* just before meals. (c) The bat has poor eyesight, but its *aural* apparatus is amazingly well developed. (d) Hearing aids can be supplied to those with *aural* defects.

4. (a) We must be careful not to let *forbearance* widen into unconcern. (b) I admired her *forbearance* in the face of the crowd's insults. (c) Great *forbearance* is needed in handling thirty children in a classroom. (d) Her *forbearance* includes a great-great-grandfather who was a general in Lincoln's army.

5. (a) He is still a young man, but his poetry has appeared in several *anthologies*. (b) I received an *anthology* of sea stories for my birthday. (c) I have several *anthologies* of British and American poetry. (d) The president was *anthologised* by everyone for his peace efforts.

6. (a) She is *preoccupied* with her plans for rebuilding the house. (b) He wore a *preoccupied* air as he listened to the music. (c) She is usually *preoccupied* as a gardener during the summer months. (d) He looked so *preoccupied* that I hated to disturb him.

7. (a) The next few years will be the most *crucial* in our nation's history. (b) Chicago plays Detroit tonight in the most *crucial* game of the season. (c) The pain was so *crucial* that sweat broke out on his brow. (d) The decision was a *crucial* one, as it would determine the winner.

8. (a) The last race was a *handicap* in which seven horses were entered. (b) The climbers *handicapped* themselves slowly up the face of the mountain. (c) She is *handicapped* by her lack of education. (d) In the afternoon the governor visited a school for *handicapped* children.

9. (a) I had forgotten how to *subjugate* the verb "to be." (b) Most of Europe was under the *subjugation* of Rome for several hundred years. (c) She was determined to *subjugate* the horse's will to her own. (d) She was asked to *subjugate* her own feelings and accept the will of the majority.

10. (a) She was caught trying to *espionage* secret information from the enemy. (b) The government is understandably reluctant to talk about its methods of *espionage*. (c) He was in *espionage* during the war. (d) Agents trained in *espionage* were dropped behind the enemy lines.

11. (a) Her knowledge of advanced mathematics will *astute* you. (b) I admire that rather *astute* study of American politics she published last year. (c) Her *astuteness* will be a great asset if she decides to run for office. (d) He *astutely* played off one opponent against the other.

12. (a) The cause of the fire has not been *ascertained*. (b) Are you absolutely *ascertain* that he did not return? (c) Did you *ascertain* the precise time she left the house? (d) There are certain tests by which you can *ascertain* the amount of metal in the ore.

13. (a) The *rift* between the two countries has

widened in the past few years. (b) A *rift* valley is formed when a strip of the earth's crust sinks between two parallel faults. (c) She was *rift* of all she possessed when her home burned down. (d) The *rift* in the tree was caused by lightning.

14. (a) We admire the *equestrian* statue of George Washington. (b) She is the leading *equestrian* in the country. (c) He is a skilled *equestrian*. (d) The *equestrian* events at the fair are always well attended.

EXERCISE 14C

Rewrite each of the sentences below, replacing the italicized word or phrase with a word from Word List 14 and writing the word in the form that fits the rest of the sentence. Use each word only once. Write your answers in the spaces provided.

1. *The art of spying on another country's secret affairs* requires a *highly-intelligent* mind.

   . . . .

   . . . .

2. Some of the children have *hearing* defects, but they are by no means deaf.

   . . . .

   . . . .

3. The invitation to the recital by the *group of eight singers* was *printed in raised letters* on a heavy white card.

   . . . .

   . . . .

4. The *split in the earth's surface* runs for hundreds of miles in a perfectly straight line.

   . . . .

   . . . .

5. One of the best tales in this *collection of stories by different authors* deals with Napoleon's attempt to *win control over Europe*.

   . . . .

   . . . .

6. Our *horse-riding* team faces a *vitally important* test when it competes with the Belgian team on Tuesday.

   . . . .

   . . . .

7. The referee showed great *patience and self-control* when he was repeatedly insulted by the crowd.

   . . . .

   . . . .

8. I will *find out* the precise nature of her *disability* for you.

   . . . .

   . . . .

9. She was too *absorbed in her own thoughts* to pay any attention to us.

   . . . .

   . . . .

EXERCISE 14D

SUBJUGATE, meaning "to conquer" or "to bring under control," comes from the Latin word *jugum* (yoke) and the Latin prefix *sub-* (under). A *subjugated* people are *under* the *yoke* of a conqueror, the yoke being a familiar symbol for slavery.

You should note that for ease in pronunciation the *b* in *sub-* often changes to agree with the first letter of the root.

Here are eight Latin words with their meanings:

mare	(sea)
cumbere	(to lie)
portare	(to carry)
figere	(to place)
terra	(earth)
pendere	(to hang)
premere	(to press)
mergere	(to plunge)

By joining the appropriate form of the Latin prefix *sub-* to roots formed from these Latin words, construct words that fit the definitions below. Check each word so formed in your dictionary for correctness and spelling.

1. to carry the weight of; to hold up

   . . . .

2. a kind of warship that can operate under the sea

   . . . .

3. to hang by a support from above

   . . . .

4. to place or sink under the surface of a liquid

   . . . .

5. to give way; to yield; to die

   . . . .

6. to put down by force

   . . . .

7. underground

   . . . .

8. a syllable or syllables added to the end of a word to alter its meaning

   . . . .

EXERCISE 14E

Write out, in the spaces provided, the words from Word List 14 for which a definition, homonym, synonym, or antonym is given. When you are asked to give a root or a prefix, you should refer back to the preceding exercise; the information you require will be found there. Make sure that each of your answers has the same number of letters as there are spaces. A definition followed by a number is a review word; the number gives the Word List from which it is taken.

If all the words are filled in correctly, the boxes running up and down the answer spaces will give you the first six words of a quotation by a great Roman statesman and philosopher. The author's name will be found at the end of the quotation which is continued in Exercise 15E.

1. the practice of one nation spying on another

2. the first eight lines of a sonnet

3. a synonym for *vital*

4. a male horseback rider

5. a nagging, scolding woman (13)

6. not fake; genuine (12)

7. showing patience and self-control

8. an antonym for *advantage*

9. a synonym for *split*

10. a collection of poems or stories by different authors

11. a synonym for *determine*

12. to conquer and bring under control

13. to make stand out from the surface

14. to make reference to (12)

15. a Latin prefix meaning "under"

16. long-lasting (7)

17. having to do with the ears or hearing

18. an antonym for *stupid*

19. a confused fight or brawl (7)

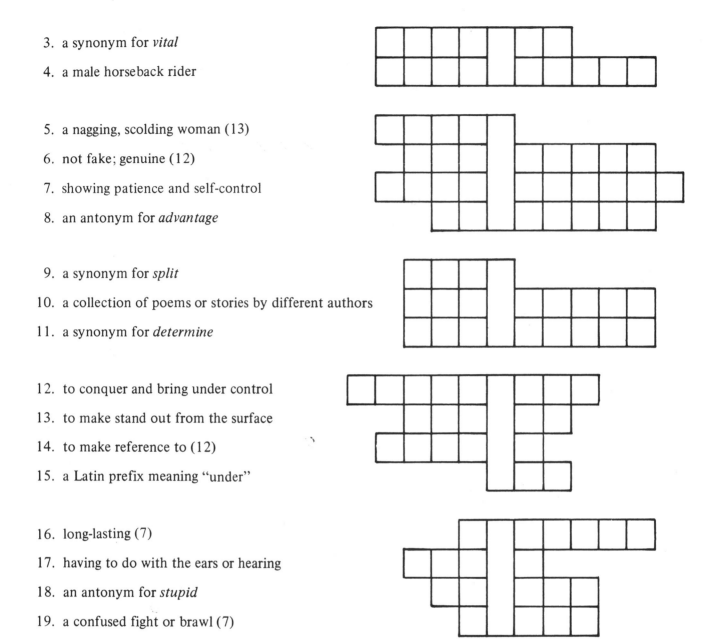

WORDLY WISE 14

A person who collects the best writings of various authors or poets and arranges them into an ANTHOLOGY could be compared to a person who collects various kinds of flowers and arranges them into a bouquet. If this comparison seems a little far-fetched, consider the origin of the word *anthology;* it comes from two Greek words, *anthos* (flower) and *lego* (gather), and literally means "a collection of flowers."

Don't confuse *oral*, which means "having to do with the mouth," with AURAL, which means "having to do with the ears or hearing." The two words are pronounced the same.

EQUESTRIAN is an adjective meaning "having to do with horses or horseback riding"; it is also a noun meaning "a male horseback rider." A female horseback rider is called an *equestrienne.*

Note that OCTET is a musical term referring to eight performers or a piece for eight performers. It is also the term for the first eight lines of a fourteen-line sonnet. Some other words from the Greek *octa* or Latin *octo* are: *octagon,* an eight-sided figure; *octave,* the eight full notes of the musical scale; *octavo,* a book size in which eight pages are printed to a sheet, usually written 8 vo; and *October,* the eighth month of the Roman calendar.

Word List 15

ADULATION	ESCAPADE	MIRE
ALMS	FESTOON	RENDEZVOUS
BAN	FORGE	RODENT
BESIEGE	INFLICT	STOCKADE
EDIT	MESA	SUBTLE
EMBALM		

Look up the words above in your dictionary. Note that some of the words have more than one meaning. When you feel that you know *all* the meanings of *all* the words, go on to the exercise below.

EXERCISE 15A

From the four choices under each phrase or sentence, you are to mark the one that is closest in meaning to the word appearing in italics. When the same word appears more than once, you should note that it is being used in a different sense.

1. a *subtle* suggestion
   (a) friendly (b) indirect (c) foolish (d) useful

2. *subtle* colors
   (a) fading (b) delicate (c) contrasting (d) strong

3. to *inflict* pain
   (a) suffer (b) fear (c) withstand (d) cause

4. to *edit* something
   (a) swallow whole (b) prepare for publication (c) publicly perform (d) practice until perfect

5. *rodent* control
   (a) fire (b) rat and mice (c) flood (d) self

6. to *besiege* the fort
   (a) rebuild from the ground up (b) surround in order to attack (c) withdraw from (d) defend to the last man

7. to *forge* ahead
   (a) move with difficulty (b) look nervously (c) plan carefully (d) leap blindly

8. to work in a *forge*

9. to *forge* a signature
   (a) imitate falsely (b) witness (c) underline heavily (d) compare with another

10. the *adulation* of the crowd
    (a) mild support (b) excessive praise (c) votes (d) goodwill

11. to climb up the side of the *mesa*
    (a) Mexican flat-roofed house (b) deep, steep-sided valley (c) conical-shaped mountain (d) large, flat-topped hill

12. to *embalm* a body
    (a) prepare for burial (b) place in a tomb (c) examine for signs of injury (d) burn on a pile of wood

13. to ask for *alms*
    (a) help from God (b) money for the poor (c) forgiveness for one's sins (d) more time

14. an opening in the *stockade*
    (a) wall made of tall stakes (b) company that trades with the natives (c) dense jungle (d) sheer rock face

15. Don't fall in the *mire!*
    (a) deep hole (b) deep mud (c) pool of water (d) small stream

16. a daring *escapade*
    (a) escape (b) remark (c) adventure (d) friend

17. to *ban* smoking on airplanes
    (a) be in favor of (b) not permit (c) be against (d) permit

18. a secret *rendezvous*
    (a) meeting (b) hiding place (c) message (d) plan

19. *festoons* around the walls
    (a) carved figures (b) wood panels (c) looped decorations (d) colored lights

(a) place where bread is baked (b) metal-working shop (c) woodworking shop (d) place where bricks are made

Check your answers against the correct ones below. The answers are not in order; this is to prevent your eye catching sight of the correct ones before you have had a chance to do the exercise on your own.

Go back to your dictionary and look up again those words for which you gave incorrect answers. Only after doing this should you go on to the next exercise.

EXERCISE 15B

Each word from Word List 15 is used four times in the sentences below; one of the sentences in each group uses the word incorrectly. You are to circle the letter that precedes that sentence. Do not circle more than one letter in any one group.

1. (a) The difference between the two proposals was too *subtle* for my mind to grasp. ● The ground beneath our feet was so *subtle* that we sank up to our ankles in it. (c) I love the *subtle* colors in his landscapes. (d) She has a *subtle* mind, and she is a hard woman to debate with.

2. (a) The box office has been *besieged* with people demanding tickets. (b) The *besiege* lasted almost a year before the town surrendered. ● The movie star and his bride were *besieged* by reporters following the ceremony. (d) The town had been *besieged* for over six months, and no relief was in sight.

3. ● The warm gulf waters are *festooned* with sharks. (b) *Festoons* of flowers and leaves were hung around the room. (c) The children were making *festoons* to string around the walls. (d) The dining hall had been *festooned* with gaily-colored paper decorations.

4. (a) The steep sides of the *mesa* rose abruptly from the desert floor. (b) Around one o'clock everyone in town settles down for an afternoon *mesa*. (c) The *mesa* was several hundred feet high and perhaps half a mile across. ●. A *mesa* consists of layers of rock that have resisted erosion.

5. ● The government is expected to lift the *ban* on exporting silver. (b) The *ban* on the sale of fireworks goes into effect tomorrow. (c) He was *banned* from leaving the country. (d) Rats have broken into the *bans* and eaten the corn.

6. ● The heavy rains have turned the football field into a *mire*. (b) I *mirely* wanted to give you a piece of advice. (c) The horses were hopelessly *mired* in the deep mud. (d) He is so *mired* in debt that he will never be able to repay what he owes.

7. (a) The stamp that I thought was worth fifty dollars turned out to be a *forge* worth maybe fifty cents. (b) He *forged* his friend's signature on the check and cashed it. ● The best swords were those *forged* in Toledo, Spain. (d) She moved into the lead and *forged* ahead to the finish line.

8. (a) Heavy losses were *inflicted* on the enemy last week. ● Do not threaten punishment you are not in a position to *inflict*. (c) You have no right to *inflict* your opinions on the rest of us. (d) She has been *inflicted* with blindness since early childhood.

9. ● She *edited* the two short ropes together to make a single long one. (b) Professor Meyer is *editing* the letters of James Boswell for publication next year. (c) Many moviemakers prefer to *edit* their own films. (d) The *editor* of the paper has the final say on what goes into it.

10. (a) Safe inside the *stockade*, the people went about their normal business. (b) A *stockade* was built around the fort to protect it from Indian attacks. (c) The prisoners soon realized there was no way to escape from the *stockade*. ● A *stockade* of shots whistled about our heads.

11. (a) They followed the *rendezvous* until it led

them to a small clearing in the woods. ● The two ships *rendezvous* at midnight. (c) They met at the *rendezvous* previously agreed upon. (d) He arranged a secret *rendezvous* with his supporters.

12. (a) Bottles of *embalm* lined the walls of the room. ● The ancient Egyptians brought *embalming* to a fine art. (c) Her memory is forever *embalmed* in the hearts of her people. (d) The body was *embalmed* by the local undertaker.

13. ● The tiny shrew and the large beaver are both members of the *rodent* family. (b) He looked *rodently* at me when I suggested dividing the money equally. (c) The front teeth of *rodents* never stop growing and are kept down to size by continual gnawing. (d) Poison is put down each night to kill *rodents*.

14. (a) The now forgotten movie star thought sadly of the *adulation* that had once been hers. (b) One may respect the woman without heaping *adulation* upon her. (c) She had not sought the *adulation* of the crowd, nor did she enjoy it. ● He *adulated* gracefully onto the platform.

15. (a) They made their way down the *escapade* that ran by the window. (b) The whole thing was a mere childish *escapade* that is best forgotten. ● The *escapade* ended when the car they had stolen crashed into a tree. (d) He was involved in one *escapade* after another as a student.

16. (a) Beggars held out their hands, asking for *alms*. (b) He owns *alms* totaling almost five million dollars. (c) *Alms* were collected in a box at the church door. ● The mere giving of *alms* does not by itself make a person holy.

EXERCISE 15C

Rewrite each of the following sentences, replacing the italicized word or phrase with a word from Word List 15 and writing the word in the form that fits the rest of the sentence. Use each word only once. Write your answers in the spaces provided.

1. The government intends to *issue an order forbidding* the sale of guns.

   . . . .

   . . . .

2. Rats and other *animals having sharp front teeth for gnawing* are said to *be the cause of* millions of dollars' worth of damage each year.

   . . . .

   . . . .

3. After the body had been *treated with chemicals to prevent it from decaying*, it was placed in the coffin.

   . . . .

   . . . .

4. The movie actress loved the *excessive praise* of the crowd and greatly enjoyed being *surrounded and eagerly questioned* by reporters wherever she went.

   . . . .

   . . . .

5. The student who *directs the publication of* the school paper was asked not to write about last night's *daring adventure*.

   . . . .

   . . . .

6. They climbed the *large, steep-sided, flat-topped outcropping of rock* and looked down on the *fort, protected by a wall of tall stakes*, that lay below.

   . . . .

7. When our carriage got stuck in the *deep, sticky mud,* I walked up the road to the blacksmith's *metalworking shop* to get help.

. . . .

. . . .

8. Her suggestion concerning the giving of *money to the poor* was expressed in an *indirect and not too obvious* manner.

. . . .

. . . .

9. The campus coffee shop, our usual *meeting place* after classes, was adorned with *large, looped decorations* for a party being given that night.

. . . .

. . . .

EXERCISE 15D

You have seen, in these exercises, that many of our words come to us from Latin or Greek. You would be wrong to think that these are the only languages from which English has taken words. To take only the words in Word List 15 as an example, we find borrowings from Spanish (MESA), Italian (FESTOON), French (RENDEZVOUS), Provencal, the language of southern France during the Middle Ages, (STOCKADE), as well as Greek (ALMS), and Latin (ADULATION, RODENT, INFLICT).

In a dictionary that gives word origins, look up the following words and give the language from which each was brought into English.

1. tea . . . .

2. tattoo . . . .

3. zinc . . . .

4. gingham . . . .

5. zero . . . .

6. ski . . . .

7. camel . . . .

8. cobra . . . .

9. horde . . . .

10. vodka . . . .

11. anthology . . . .

12. cruise . . . .

13. clarity . . . .

14. motto . . . .

15. tulip . . . .

16. cigar . . . .

17. espionage . . . .

18. bungalow . . . .

EXERCISE 15E

Write out, in the spaces provided, the words from Word List 15 for which a definition, homonym, synonym, or antonym is given. When you are asked to give a root or a prefix, you should refer back to the preceding exercise; the information you require will be found there. Make sure that each of your answers has the same number of letters as there are spaces. A definition followed by a number is a review word; the number gives the Word List from which it is taken.

If all the words are filled in correctly, the boxes running up and down the answer spaces will continue the quotation begun earlier.

1. a synonym for *adventure*

2. an area of muddy or marshy ground

3. an antonym for *scorn*

4. a synonym for *forbid*

5. an animal with sharp front teeth used for gnawing
6. a collection of poems or short stories by different authors (14)
7. to treat (a body) with chemicals to prevent decay
8. an antonym for *obvious*

9. a decoration of looped flowers or paper

10. to fascinate (7)

11. a large, steep-sided, flat-topped hill

12. a wide tidal mouth of a river (8)

13. a protective wall of tall stakes

14. to shape (metal) by heating and pounding

15. to impose or put upon as a punishment

16. a synonym for *meeting*

17. to surround and attack

18. a period in history (6)

19. to prepare for publication

20. money or other help given to the poor

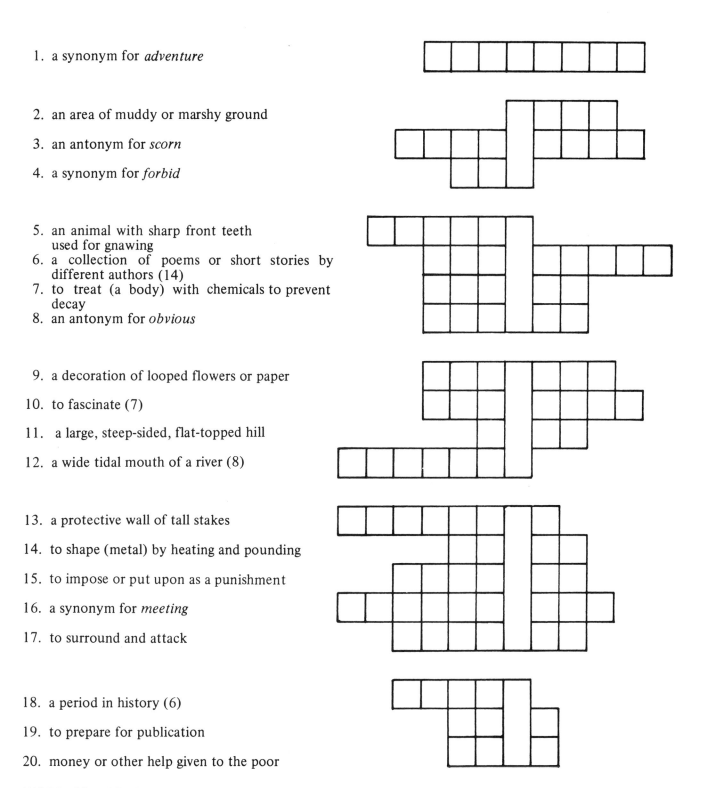

WORDLY WISE 15

A few notes on pronunciation: SUBTLE is pronounced *SUT–'l;* RENDEZVOUS (a word borrowed from the French) is pronounced *RON–day–voo;* ALMS is pronounced *ahms.*

To *afflict* is to distress with mental or bodily suffering, to trouble greatly; to INFLICT is to impose or lay on something unwelcome. It is easy to confuse these two words; perhaps this sentence will illustrate the difference between them. "Although he was *afflicted* with weak eyesight, he managed to *inflict* several blows on the boy who attacked them."

ACROSS

1. a forewarning
4. not simple; complex (11)
6. to make a raised pattern on
8. having grave or important results
10. to give off smoke
12. to work together on something
13. a difficulty that cannot be solved
14. to forbid by law
17. supernatural; weird
19. a protective wall of high stakes
20. a section in a speech or written piece
21. a gnawing animal with sharp teeth
22. to cause, as damage or pain
24. of horses or horseback riders
28. a swamp or bog
30. a small amount
31. a daring prank
34. to prepare for publication
36. to surround and attack
38. to make worse
39. very eager; enthusiastic (11)
41. a collection of poems
42. high praise or flattery
43. to make known
44. to move back (3)
45. strange (3)

DOWN

1. absorbed in something else
2. to prepare a body for burial
3. a group of eight
4. very important; critical
5. money given to the poor
7. to conquer
8. to shape metal with heat
9. to pass or slip by, as time (1)
10. to decorate with loops of flowers
11. to hinder
15. a small, mouse-like animal
16. to figure out; determine
18. of the ears or hearing
23. patience; restraint
25. a meeting
26. to overstate
27. the act of spying
28. a steep, flat-topped hill
29. a mass of sliding snow or rocks
32. a person to whom one owes money
33. to refrain from; hold back
35. to flatter excessively
37. not easily seen or understood
38. clever; wise
40. a split or crack

88

Chapter Six

Word List 16

CLERICAL	PLUMB	TENEMENT
COGITATE	RANDOM	TICK
CONTEMPT	RESPLENDENT	TOPICAL
IMPERTINENT	SHANTY	VAGUE
PENNANT	SLAKE	

Look up the words above in your dictionary. Note that some of the words have more than one meaning. When you feel that you know *all* the meanings of *all* the words, go on to the exercise below.

EXERCISE 16A

From the four choices under each phrase or sentence, you are to mark the one that is closest in meaning to the word appearing in italics. When the same word appears more than once, you should note that it is being used in a different sense.

1. subjects that are *topical*
   (a) forbidden to be discussed (b) in the news (c) required to be covered (d) outdated

2. a *random* selection
   (a) precisely arranged (b) fair (c) by chance (d) wide-ranging

3. a *plumb* line
   (a) thin (b) broken (c) weighted (d) curved

4. to *plumb* the mystery
   (a) be mystified by (b) attempt to complicate (c) be the cause of (d) get to the bottom of

5. to *cogitate* for a moment
   (a) wait (b) think deeply (c) hesitate (d) panic

6. to feel *contempt*
   (a) sadness (b) joy (c) scorn (d) uneasiness

7. to *slake* one's thirst
   (a) be unable to satisfy (b) look forward to satisfying (c) satisfy (d) increase

8. *clerical* duties
   (a) tiresome (b) enjoyable (c) priestly (d) political

9. *clerical* work
   (a) easy (b) office (c) farm (d) unpleasant

10. an old *shanty*
    (a) crudely-built hut (b) gossipy man (c) tomcat (d) wise woman

11. a *resplendent* figure
    (a) ridiculous (b) bent (c) pathetic (d) dazzling

12. a striped *tick*
    (a) pillow cover (b) handkerchief (c) scarf (d) tablecloth

13. infested with *ticks*
    (a) animals that resemble mice (b) small, harmless snakes (c) bloodsucking bugs (d) people who are not wanted

14. Put a *tick* against one's name.
    (a) √ (b) X (c) ? (d) *

15. a crowded *tenement*
    (a) self-service restaurant (b) run-down apartment building (c) city square (d) public hall

16. a blue *pennant*
    (a) triangular flag (b) three-cornered hat (c) triangular scarf (d) headband

17. a *vague* answer
    (a) exact (b) unclear (c) carefully thought out (d) surprising

18. an *impertinent* child
    (a) rude (b) silent (c) careless (d) sickly

Check your answers against the correct ones at the top of the next page. The answers are not in order; this is to prevent your eye catching sight of the correct ones before you have had a chance to do the exercise on your own.

12a. 6c. 11d. 7c. 9b. 16a. 2c. 10a. 17b. 1b. 5b. 15b. 4d. 14a. 8c. 18a. 13c. 3c.

Go back to your dictionary and look up again those words for which you gave incorrect answers. Only after doing this should you go on to the next exercise.

EXERCISE 16B

Each word from Word List 16 is used four times in the sentences below; one of the sentences in each group uses the word incorrectly. You are to circle the letter that precedes that sentence. Do not circle more than one letter in any one group.

1. (a) They fired a few *random* shots to frighten the intruders. (b) The numbers were chosen at *random*. (c) The king had to pay a heavy *random* to free his son. (d) There was a *random* assortment of brooches, ribbons, clips, and other articles.

2. (a) After considerable *cogitation* they agreed on a plan. (b) The two wheels are not *cogitating* together properly because one of them is loose. (c) The three members silently *cogitated* the problem. (d) She sat and *cogitated* for a minute before answering.

3. (a) We saw the *vague* outline of a ship looming out of the fog. (b) They talked *vaguely* about the need to do something. (c) Her memory began to *vague* as she got older. (d) She had only a *vague* idea of what she wanted.

4. (a) The court can *contempt* him for up to thirty days. (b) He was given thirty days by the judge for *contempt* of court. (c) She looked with *contempt* at us when we refused to help. (d) The acts of these traitors bring our nation into *contempt*.

5. (a) "You've got an ugly face," he said *impertinently*. (b) Such *impertinence* must not go

unpunished. (c) The wine had an *impertinent* taste, probably because it had been left uncorked. (d) He was *impertinent* enough to ask how much money I owed.

6. (a) Use a *plumb* line to make sure the walls are vertical. (b) The governor had a judgeship and a few other political *plumbs* at her disposal. (c) The pipe was sealed with a *plumb* joint. (d) That man has *plumbed* the very depths of despair.

7. (a) The admiral's *pennant* fluttered from the flagpole. (b) He was required to fast for three days as a *pennant* for his sins. (c) The store was decorated with rows of brightly-colored *pennants*. (d) It had been ten years since the team had won the *pennant*.

8. (a) Before these buildings were put up, this area was a *shanty*town. (b) The house had grown *shanty* with age and needed to be pulled down. (c) O'Donnell said he was proud of being descended from the *shanty* Irish. (d) The old man lived in a *shanty* by the side of the lake.

9. (a) He touched on air pollution, our crowded cities, and other *topical* issues. (b) Each student should hand in a *topical* outline of his research paper. (c) Damp, foggy weather is *topical* of this region. (d) She told a few *topical* jokes that were well received.

10. (a) She was anxious to know what had happened, but I did nothing to *slake* her curiosity. (b) We *slaked* our dry throats with melted snow. (c) A mixture of sand and *slaked* lime is needed to make concrete. (d) The little mountain stream *slaked* its way between the rocks.

11. (a) The Black Prince was *resplendent* in shining armor. (b) She wore a jeweled *resplendent* around her neck. (c) The monarch butterfly is a truly *resplendent* creature. (d) The moon in all its *resplendent* glory shone

down upon the ocean.

12. (a) The sheep are dipped in a special solution to kill *ticks*. (b) She had a slight facial *tick* which caused her mouth to twitch rather oddly. (c) We listened to the clock *tick* away the minutes. (d) Put a *tick* against the name of anyone who is late.

13. (a) The minister always wore his *clerical* collar. (b) Typists and other *clerical* workers are demanding equal pay with factory workers. (c) He works as a *clerical* in the office next door. (d) She was a member of the clergy who tried to live up to her *clerical* vows.

14. (a) The house was *tenemented* by a family from Chicago. (b) There was a vacant second-floor *tenement* for rent for fifty dollars a month. (c) He looked gloomily at the row of drab *tenements*. (d) These *tenement* houses were once the mansions of city merchants.

EXERCISE 16C

Rewrite each of the sentences below, replacing the italicized word or phrase with a word from Word List 16 and writing the word in the form that fits the rest of the sentence. Use each word only once. Write your answers in the spaces provided.

1. The effect of computers on *clerks and other office* workers is a subject that is *currently in the news.*

   . . . .

   . . . .

2. Outside the *crudely built hut* was a faucet at which I was able to *satisfy* my thirst.

   . . . .

   . . . .

3. After *thinking deeply* for a few moments, Sherlock Holmes said, "I have *gotten to the bottom of* the mystery."

   . . . .

   . . . .

4. The yacht, *bright and shining* in the sunlight, moved out of the harbor, its blue *triangular flag* fluttering in the breeze.

   . . . .

   . . . .

5. If any girl is *deliberately failing to show proper respect* to you, put a *small check mark* against her name in the punishment book.

   . . . .

   . . . .

6. The selection of the twelve people was *made entirely by chance,* so naturally they were *rather uncertain* when asked why they had been chosen.

   . . . .

   . . . .

7. There is no reason why people who live in *old, crowded apartment buildings in the slums* should be held in *low esteem* by those who are more fortunate.

   . . . .

   . . . .

EXERCISE 16D

Suffixes seldom change the essential meaning of a word, but they do change the form. For example, by adding the suffix *-ly* to the adjective IMPERTINENT, we form the adverb *impertinently;* by changing the suffix from *-ent* to *-ence,* we form the noun *impertinence.*

Complete the words in the following sentences

by filling in the appropriate suffix. In the space provided after each sentence, write out whether the suffix forms a verb, a noun, an adverb, or an adjective.

1. No one knows the destruct . . . . power of the bomb. (   )

2. The bomb caused great destruct . . . . (   )

3. The army decided to mechan . . . . the cavalry. (   )

4. He built a mechan . . . . man in his workshop. (   )

5. She wants to be a mechan . . . . . ( )

6. She offered to test . . . . in court. ( )

7. Her testi . . . . impressed the jury. ( )

8. Do you real . . . . what you have done? (   )

9. Her dream of fame became a real . . . . . (   )

10. Are you real . . . . . sure that this is what you want? (   )

EXERCISE 16E

Write out, in the spaces provided, the words from Word List 16 for which a definition, homonym, synonym, or antonym is given on the next page. When you are asked to give a root or a prefix, you should refer back to the preceding exercise; the information you require will be found there. Make sure that each of your answers has the same number of letters as there are spaces. A definition followed by a number is a review word; the number gives the Word List from which it is taken.

If all the words are filled in correctly, the boxes running up and down the answer spaces will continue the quotation begun earlier.

1. the cloth case or cover of a pillow or mattress

2. a crowded, run-down city apartment building

3. a synonym for *think*

4. a gnawing animal, as a rat, beaver, or squirrel (15)

5. an antonym for *polite*

6. a collection of poems or stories by different writers (14)

7. an antonym for *drab*

8. a lead weight attached to a line for finding depths

9. having to do with priests or the clergy

10. a person to whom one owes money (13)

11. able to produce the desired result (11)

12. an antonym for *distinct*

13. to satisfy, as a thirst

14. a crudely made hut or small house

15. currently in the news

16. done in an aimless way without planning

17. a flag that is won by a championship team

18. an antonym for *respect*

19. to make senseless or dull-witted (5)

WORDLY WISE 16

A PLUMB is a lead weight hung at the end of a line. It is used to find out how deep water is or whether a wall is straight up and down. The word comes from the Latin *plumbum*, which means "lead." *Plumber* comes from the same source, for bathroom and kitchen pipes and joints were once made of lead; so does *plummet*, which means "to fall directly to earth." It is not difficult to see how the verb *plumb*, which means "to measure depth with a plumb line," came also to mean "to get to the bottom of" in the sense of "to solve."

A TENEMENT is a run-down, crowded apartment building; but note that a suite of rooms or apartment rented by the week or the month is also called a tenement.

Word List 17

ABOUND	ELOPE	NAIVETÉ
ANNIHILATE	EXPANSIVE	OGRE
BIGAMY	INARTICULATE	PANDEMONIUM
CONSIDER	INITIATIVE	RANKLE
DIALECT	LAMINATED	TOKEN

Look up the words above in your dictionary. Note that some of the words have more than one meaning. When you feel that you know *all* the meanings of *all* the words, go on to the exercise below.

EXERCISE 17A

From the four choices under each phrase or sentence, you are to mark the one that is closest in meaning to the word appearing in italics. When the same word appears more than once, you should note that it is being used in a different sense.

1. to take the *initiative*
   (a) money set aside for something (b) blame (c) first step (d) credit

2. He has *initiative.*
   (a) the ability to get things done (b) an ample supply of cash (c) a warm and friendly manner (d) friends with influence

3. to *annihilate* a city
   (a) destroy completely (b) surround and attack (c) know thoroughly (d) move out of

4. It *rankles.*
   (a) doesn't stay neat and pressed (b) begins to come loose or fall apart (c) causes a lasting bitterness (d) fails to work properly

5. We plan to *elope.*
   (a) go on a long vacation (b) exchange letters (c) keep a record of progress (d) run away to be married

6. an *ogre* in a fairy tale
   (a) friendly elf (b) fairy godmother (c) beautiful princess (d) hideous, man-eating giant

7. He's such an *ogre.*
   (a) kind old man (b) unpleasant man (c) well-meaning man (d) foolish man

8. to *consider* the question
   (a) repeat (b) answer (c) think about (d) forget for a moment

9. to *consider* the feelings of others
   (a) be unconcerned about (b) be ignorant of (c) be mindful of (d) play upon

10. *Pandemonium* broke out.
    (a) loud sobbing (b) great disorder (c) general laughter (d) heated arguments

11. the crime of *bigamy*
    (a) stealing from one's employer (b) betraying one's country (c) falsely signing someone's name (d) marrying while already married

12. to show great *naiveté*
    (a) anger (b) pride in oneself (c) innocence (d) interest

13. Wild animals *abound.*
    (a) leap and frolic (b) are kept in cages (c) exist in large numbers (d) run free

14. *abounding* confidence
    (a) great (b) pretended (c) lacking (d) justified

15. a *token* of authority
    (a) fear (b) love (c) sign (d) withdrawing

16. A *token* costs thirty cents.
    (a) one-way fare (b) little plastic toy (c) metal disk used in place of money (d) small ribbon to put on one's hat

17. to be *inarticulate*
    (a) poorly proportioned (b) mistrusted (c) clumsy in movement (d) unable to speak

18. *expansive* fields
    (a) highly-productive (b) uncultivated (c) with many hills and valleys (d) covering a large area

19. to grow *expansive*
    (a) fat (b) sullen (c) suspicious (d) friendly

20. All cards should be *laminated.*
    (a) made out correctly (b) covered with plastic (c) renewed when becoming out of date (d) kept handy at all times

21. *laminated* wood
    (a) roughly-finished (b) squared-off (c) layered (d) highly-polished

22. a strange *dialect*
    (a) part of a country (b) crime for which there is no motive (c) passage in a play (d) regional form of a language

Check your answers against the correct ones below. The answers are not in order; this is to prevent your eye catching sight of the correct ones before you have had a chance to do the exercise on your own.

12c. 6d. 19d. 11d. 7b. 20b. 9c. 16c. 21c. 2a. 10b. 17d. 1c. 22d. 5d. 15c. 4c. 13c. 8c. 18d. 14a. 3a.

Go back to your dictionary and look up again those words for which you gave incorrect answers. Only after doing this should you go on to the next exercise.

EXERCISE 17B

Each word from Word List 17 is used four times in the following sentences; one of the sentences in each group uses the word incorrectly. You are to circle the letter that precedes that sentence. Do not circle more than one letter in any one group.

1. (a) He finds it very hard to *inarticulate* properly. (b) He gave an *inarticulate* grunt when I spoke to him. (c) She was almost *inarticulate* with rage. (d) She speaks for the *inarticulate* masses.

2. (a) The fairy tale tells how the *ogre* lured people into his castle. (b) These delays do not *ogre* well for the success of the project. (c) They say that the manager is an *ogre* to work for, but I have always found him easy to get along with. (d) The *ogress* in the fairy tale said she was going to eat the small child.

3. (a) She was *considering* my offer when the telephone rang. (b) He added a *consider* to the effect that he would not be responsible. (c) She is generally *considered* a wise ruler. (d) He *considered* the wishes of his parents in everything he did.

4. (a) Hatred *rankled* in his heart. (b) They *rankled* among themselves as to who should go first. (c) The punishment he had received *rankled* as an act of great injustice. (d) Having to pay more than the market price *rankled* her.

5. (a) The fifty soldiers were a *token* force only and were far fewer than were needed. (b) She *tokened* to me to follow her. (c) He gave her a ring as a *token* of his love. (d) To enter the subway, you must put a *token* in the turnstile.

6. (a) Shale is made of *laminated* clay and can be split very easily. (b) The natives *laminated* the death of their chief. (c) His identification card was *laminated* between sheets of plastic. (d) *Laminated* wood is very strong.

7. (a) They were *eloped* by the parish priest the next morning. (b) Both their parents wanted a big wedding, but they decided to *elope*. (c) She tried to *elope* but was caught and brought back by her father. (d) Following their *elopement*, the two young people moved to California.

8. (a) The king was *annihilated* by a sniper in one of the buildings. (b) The townspeople were told that their city would be *annihilated* unless they surrendered. (c) Following the complete *annihilation* of the army, the general went into voluntary exile. (d) The systematic *annihilation* of the buffalo is one of this country's great tragedies.

9. (a) We quickly took the *initiative* and went on

to an easy victory. (b) We need a leader who possesses *initiative* and imagination. (c) They promised that her *initiative* into the sorority would take place soon. (d) She acted entirely on her own *initiative* in this matter.

10. (a) He grew *expansive* over dinner and talked amusingly of his experiences. (b) Her talk is on the religions of the world or something equally *expansive*. (c) Thirty dollars a day is too *expansive* for a single room. (d) In chemistry we tested the *expansive* properties of gases when heated.

11. (a) He answered *bigamously* when asked what he did for a living. (b) He was convicted of *bigamy* and jailed for five years. (c) She claimed to be the man's real wife and accused him of being a *bigamist*. (d) It was several years before she discovered that her marriage was *bigamous*.

12. (a) The roof and the sides were covered with strips of *pandemonium*. (b) The shouting and the excitement grew to a *pandemonium*. (c) *Pandemonium* broke out when the white mice escaped during the science class. (d) By the time his speech was finished, the hall was in *pandemonium*.

13. (a) It is *naiveté* of you to believe everything you are told. (b) Although wise in the ways of the city, she had an air of *naiveté* that was charming. (c) His *naiveté* in business matters is well known. (d) Children have a *naiveté* that adults find quite touching.

14. (a) The dog came *abounding* into the room, its tail wagging furiously. (b) He has *abounding* confidence in his ability to succeed. (c) The woods *abound* with animals of every kind. (d) The city of Rome *abounds* in historical buildings.

15. (a) Robert Burns wrote his poetry in the *dialect* of his native Scotland. (b) She is here to study the *dialects* of the South. (c) The essay is in the form of a *dialect* between two philosophers. (d) Attic, Ionian, Doric, and Aeolic are *dialects* of ancient Greek.

EXERCISE 17C

Rewrite each of the sentences below, replacing the italicized word or phrase with a word from Word List 17 and writing the word in the form that fits the rest of the sentence. Use each word only once. Write your answers in the spaces provided.

1. Since fish *are to be found in large numbers* in these lakes, I wish you would *think seriously about* my suggestion that we go fishing.

   . . . .

   . . . .

2. The fact that her daughter *ran away from home to get married* still *causes a feeling of great bitterness*.

   . . . .

   . . . .

3. At first I thought her *unable to speak for some reason,* but over dinner she became quite *friendly and eager to talk*.

   . . . .

   . . . .

4. His *lack of knowledge of the ways of the world* is so great that he actually seemed surprised when I explained that *going through a form of marriage while already married* is a crime.

   . . . .

   . . . .

5. Once upon a time there was a *hideous giant* who just loved eating little children!

   . . . .

6. The *metal disks used in place of money* on the buses and subways are made of two different metals *formed in layers and pressed* together.

. . . .

. . . .

7. She is an expert on *forms of the language that are spoken only in certain parts of the country.*

. . . .

. . . .

8. Miguel certainly showed *an ability to do things on his own* when he started that little business.

. . . .

. . . .

9. *Great confusion and disorder* broke out in the city when the invading army at the gates threatened to *completely destroy* it.

. . . .

. . . .

EXERCISE 17D

John Milton, the great English poet, in his epic **Paradise Lost,** coined the word PANDEMONIUM by combining the two Greek words *pan* (all) and *daemon* (devil or demon). *Pandemonium* was the place where *all* the *devils* lived.

The Latin equivalent of *pan* is *omni,* which also means "all." Both of these words occur as roots in a number of English words.

Complete the following words, for which other roots and suffixes have been supplied, by filling in the blank space with either the Greek or the Latin root that means "all." Write out a brief definition of each word and check both word and definition in your dictionary for accuracy and spelling.

1. _____ theon

. . . .

2. _____ bus

. . . .

3. _____ acea

. . . .

4. _____ potent

. . . .

5. _____ -American

. . . .

6. _____ scient

. . . .

7. _____ chromatic

. . . .

8. _____ vorous

. . . .

9. _____ present

. . . .

10. _____ orama

. . . .

11. _____ tomime

. . . .

12. _____ theism

. . . .

EXERCISE 17E

Write out, in the spaces provided, the words from Word List 17 for which a definition, homonym, synonym, or antonym is given below. When you are asked to give a root or a prefix, you should refer back to the preceding exercise; the information you require will be found there. Make sure that each of your answers has the same number of letters as there are spaces. A definition followed by a number is a review word; the number gives the Word List from which it is taken.

If all the words are filled in correctly, the boxes running up and down the answer spaces will conclude the quotation begun earlier.

1. spread over a wide area; broad

2. a regional form of a language

3. to wipe out; to destroy utterly

4. to occur in large numbers

5. a Latin root meaning "all"

6. to cause a prolonged feeling of bitterness

7. great confusion and disorder

8. the crime of marrying while already married

9. to hang with looped decorations (15)

10. the first step in bringing something about

11. a synonym for *keepsake*

12. a man-eating giant in fairy tales

Here is the name
of the author:

13. a synonym for *reflect*

14. to run away from home to marry

15. a Greek root meaning "all"

16. childish inexperience

17. unable to speak clearly

18. made in layers

WORDLY WISE 17

BIGAMY is the crime of marrying while already married; it means, in fact, having two wives or two husbands at the same time. *Gamos* is the Greek word for "marriage," and you should remember from Exercise 12D that *bi-* is a Greek prefix meaning "two." Perhaps you can figure out the meanings of *monogamy* and (if we tell you that *poly* is a Greek prefix meaning "many") *polygamy*.

A DIALECT is a form of a language spoken only in certain parts of a country. That the United States has *dialects* becomes obvious if you try to imagine a conversation between a New York cabdriver and an old Virginia planter. In fact, this country has seven distinct *dialects:* (1) the Eastern New England dialect centered around Boston, (2) the New York City dialect, (3) the Middle Atlantic dialect centered around Philadelphia, (4) the Western Pennsylvania dialect, (5) the Southern Mountain dialect, taking in Kentucky, Tennessee, West Virginia, and parts of Virginia and North Carolina, (6) the Southern dialect, (7) the general American dialect which covers the whole of the United States west of a line drawn from Lake Ontario to Texas.

WORD LIST 18

DEPLORE	LUCID	SCRUPULOUS
DISCRETION	PERT	SPASMODIC
DUB	PROCEEDS	SUSCEPTIBLE
IMPOUND	ROTARY	UNILATERAL
INTRICATE	SALVAGE	VOLUPTUOUS

Look up the words above in your dictionary. Note that some of the words have more than one meaning. When you feel that you know *all* the meanings of *all* the words, go on to the following exercise.

EXERCISE 18A

From the four choices under each phrase or sentence, you are to mark the one that is closest in meaning to the word appearing in italics. When the same words appears more than once, you should note that it is being used in a different sense.

1. a *lucid* statement
   (a) brief (b) confusing (c) clear (d) understood

2. *susceptible to* a disease
   (a) recovering from (b) easily affected by (c) free of (d) stricken by

3. a *susceptible* person
   (a) soft-spoken (b) rude and friendly (c) easily influenced (d) easily angered

4. She *dubbed* him "The Duke."
   (a) pretended to believe (b) thought (c) offered (d) named

5. to *dub* a movie
   (a) put up the money for (b) add a sound track to (c) give a title to (d) roundly criticize

6. *spasmodic* attempts
   (a) vain (b) intermittent (c) serious (d) half-hearted

7. *spasmodic* movements
   (a) barely noticeable (b) sudden and irregular (c) gently rolling (d) slow and painful

8. a *rotary* movement
   (a) circular (b) swift (c) dangerous (d) backward and forward

9. an *intricate* design
   (a) simple (b) complicated (c) raised (d) colorful

10. Use your *discretion.*
    (a) muscle power (b) position of authority (c) charm and good looks (d) judgment

11. to show *discretion*
    (a) hatred for other people (b) care in what one says and does (c) anger over what someone says (d) a complete lack of interest

12. to *deplore* poverty
    (a) be unable to escape from (b) feel great regret about (c) try to overcome (d) study the conditions of

13. a *pert* reply
    (a) saucy (b) polite (c) unexpected (d) thoughtless

14. to *impound* the dog
(a) give away (b) shut up in an enclosure (c) keep searching for (d) raise from a puppy

15. They *impounded* his car.
(a) knocked out the dents in (b) changed the appearance of (c) seized and held (d) examined very carefully

16. to *salvage* the ship
(a) steer through difficult waters (b) refit completely (c) sink deliberately (d) save from being wrecked

17. a *unilateral* decision
(a) involving the whole world (b) final (c) private (d) involving one side only

18. *scrupulous* in his business dealings
(a) having little regard for the law (b) showing a complete lack of ability (c) being too trusting (d) careful to do what is proper

19. *voluptuous* delights
(a) imagined but not experienced (b) leading to one's undoing (c) that quickly turn sour (d) giving pleasure through the senses

20. The *proceeds* go to charity.
(a) profits from some activity (b) articles that are collected (c) sums of money left in a will (d) leftover food

Check your answers against the correct ones below. The answers are not in order; this is to prevent your eye catching sight of the correct ones before you have had a chance to do the exercise on your own.

12b. 6b. 11b. 7b. 19d. 9b. 16d. 2b. 10d. 20a. 17d. 1c. 5b. 15c. 4d. 13a. 8a. 18d. 14b. 3c.

Go back to your dictionary and look up again those words for which you gave incorrect answers. Only after doing this should you go on to the next exercise.

EXERCISE 18B

Each word from Word List 18 is used four times in the sentences below; one of the sentences in each group uses the word incorrectly. You are to circle the letter that precedes that sentence. Do not circle more than one letter in any one group.

1. (a) The *proceeds* were divided equally between the two groups. (b) I didn't have enough *proceeds* to buy a ticket. (c) She used the *proceeds* from the sale of her house to go into business. (d) The *proceeds* from the concert will be used to buy instruments for the band.

2. (a) She *impounded* at length on the importance of regular fire drills. (b) His job was to *impound* the stray dogs of the town. (c) All slave ships that put into the Bahama ports were *impounded* and their cargoes freed. (d) All records of his company have been *impounded* by the police and will be used as evidence.

3. (a) By putting a little money away each week, she soon had *salvaged* enough to buy a bicycle. (b) Material *salvaged* from the wreckage of the plane is being carefully examined. (c) The therapist has *salvaged* a number of marriages that seemed headed for divorce. (d) *Salvage* from the sunken ship was stacked alongside the dock.

4. (a) This country cannot agree to disarm *unilaterally*. (b) The *unilateral* goes into effect as soon as the president signs it. (c) The contract is a *unilateral* one, binding on one party only. (d) South Africa decided *unilaterally* to end the treaty with Spain.

5. (a) Use your own *discretion* in deciding how much to tell her. (b) You may rely on her *discretion* in this matter. (c) I have complete *discretion* in his ability to do the right thing. (d) The president has the *discretionary* power to grant pardons.

6. (a) Attempts to deal with the problem have been *spasmodic* and doomed to failure. (b) He

lay on the floor, his body twitching *spasmodically*. (c) We ran for the doctor when she began to *spasmodic*. (d) The growth of our cities has been *spasmodic* and unattended by any planning.

7. (a) She expresses herself very *lucidly*. (b) We bathed in the *lucid* waters of the pool. (c) She spoke with great *lucidity* of the needs of our cities. (d) He makes a living by carving figures out of pieces of *lucid*.

8. (a) The pool was *rotary* in shape. (b) The blades of an eggbeater have a *rotary* action. (c) *Rotary* blades drive air through the wind tunnel. (d) A hole was made in the rock with a *rotary* drill.

9. (a) The problem is *susceptible* to a solution if we all put our minds to it. (b) He claimed he was *susceptible* to colds and could not go out in damp weather. (c) She was *susceptible* that it would help, but she was willing to try it. (d) The *susceptibility* of the city to attack was a source of great concern.

10. (a) The queen *dubbed* him a knight by tapping him on the shoulder with her sword. (b) He was immediately *dubbed* "Shorty" by his classmates. (c) The soldiers *dubbed* their faces with mud so that they would not be seen. (d) The movie had been very badly *dubbed*.

11. (a) Spaceships must travel *voluptuous* distances to reach the planets. (b) The music swelled *voluptuously* before fading into silence. (c) She rose from her seat on the *voluptuous* couch to meet her guest. (d) His life was given over to the *voluptuous* pleasures of the table.

12. (a) The maze had many *intricate* passageways. (b) We were unable to *intricate* ourselves from the mire. (c) He promised to explain some of the *intricacies* of the game. (d) She has an *intricate* knowledge of the game.

13. (a) We were afraid that Jane's fever might turn *scrupulous*, so we called the doctor. (b) He is

scrupulously honest. (c) She kept a *scrupulous* account of every penny she spent. (d) He keeps the place *scrupulously* clean.

14. (a) Everyone was amused by the boy's *pert* answer. (b) They went fishing for salmon but caught only a few *pert*. (c) With a *pert* toss of her head, she ran out of the room. (d) He wore a *pert* little hat atop his curls.

15. (a) We all *deplore* the fact that he died at such an early age. (b) She *deplored* the king to release her son. (c) Conditions in the prisons were *deplorable*. (d) He *deplores* the use of slang by young people.

EXERCISE 18C

Rewrite each of the sentences below, replacing the italicized word or phrase with a word from Word List 18 and writing the word in the form that fits the rest of the sentence. Use each word only once. Write your answers in the spaces provided.

1. I *view with great sadness and regret* the fact that this country has agreed to ban nuclear weapons *without requiring other nations to do likewise.*

. . . .

. . . .

2. His sleep was broken by *sudden, sharp, and irregular* coughing throughout the night.

. . . .

. . . .

3. The blades of this power mower are *made to turn in a circle about a central point.*

. . . .

. . . .

4. Use your own *judgment* in deciding what to

do with the *profits made* from the concert.

. . . .

. . . .

5. A person using his car for smuggling risks having it *seized and held in the custody of the law.*

. . . .

. . . .

6. She has a *very detailed* knowledge of the law, and she gave a *clear* account of how the jury system works.

. . . .

. . . .

7. Because of his small size and *bold and saucy* manner, he was *given the name of* "The Sparrow."

. . . .

. . . .

8. We learned later that the blue velvet sofa cushions, which are so *pleasing and delightful to the senses,* are especially *responsive to the influence* of water marks.

. . . .

. . . .

9. Before the *property saved from the sinking ship* can be returned to the owners, a *most careful and thorough* record has to be made of every item.

. . . .

. . . .

EXERCISE 18D

Follow the directions for each of these exercises.

1. (a) Give two English words containing the Greek root that means "time."

—————————— ——————————

(b) Give two English words containing the Latin root that means "time."

—————————— ——————————

2. From which language has each of the following words been brought into English?

gingham (   )   cruise (   )
motto (   )   ski (   )
cobra (   )   cigar (   )
tea (   )   tulip (   )
zinc (   )

3. Write four words derived from the Latin root that means "water."

—————————— ——————————

—————————— ——————————

4. Give two English words containing the Greek root that means "all."

—————————— ——————————

(b) Give two words containing the Latin root that means "all."

—————————— ——————————

5. Underline the prefix in each of the following words and give its meaning.

exceptional (   )   pentagon (   )
subjugate (   )   premonition (   )
bicycle (   )   hemisphere (   )

EXERCISE 18E

Write out, in the spaces provided, the words from Word List 18 for which a definition, homonym, synonym, or antonym is given. When you are asked to give a root or a prefix, you should refer back to the preceding exercise; the information you require will be found there. Make sure that each of your answers has the same number of letters as there are spaces. A definition followed by a number is a review word; the number gives the Word List from which it is taken.

If all the words are filled in correctly, the boxes running up and down the answer spaces will give

you the first five words of a poem which will be
continued in Exercise 19E.

1. receiving, giving, or seeking pleasure
   through the senses
2. to destroy completely (17)

3. an antonym for *shy*

4. to cause, as by striking; to make suffer (15)

5. the profit made from some activity

6. affecting only one of two or more parties

7. an antonym for *careless*

8. turning in a circle around a central point

9. a scolding, nagging woman (13)

10. the ability to do things on one's own (17)

11. to seize and take into the custody
    of the law

12. having feelings that are easily affected

13. a crudely built hut or small house (16)

14. the act of spying on another country's secrets (14)

15. occurring suddenly, sharply, and irregularly

16. anything saved, as from a fire or a shipwreck

17. an antonym for *murky*

18. an antonym for *simple*

19. to willingly forego or do without (13)

20. to feel or show deep regret over

21. a synonym for *judgment*

PROCEEDS is a plural noun having no singular. (The proceeds *have* been spent.) *Proceed* is a verb that has an altogether different meaning.

Circular suggests *shape*, specifically that of a circle; ROTARY suggests *movement*, specifically along a circular path. A *circular* saw has a *rotary* motion.

Knowing that UNILATERAL means "affecting only one of several persons, parties, or nations," you should have no difficulty in figuring out the meanings of *bilateral* and (if we tell you that *multi-* is a Latin prefix meaning "many") *multilateral.* All three words occur frequently in newspaper accounts dealing with international affairs.

ACROSS

1. to think deeply
4. careful about details
10. a lead weight on a string
11. to run away secretly to marry
12. a long, triangular flag
13. a cruel and ugly man
14. speaking unclearly
15. to express deep regret about
20. to wipe out completely
22. great noise and disorder
25. a person to whom one owes money (13)
28. to cause a continual bitter feeling
29. occurring suddenly and irregularly
31. to do without (13)
33. not hurt or harmed (10)
36. giving pleasure through the senses
37. clear; easy to understand
41. inexperience; a natural simplicity
42. very sensitive; easily influenced
43. bold and saucy
44. to take away and hold
45. showing a frank and open manner; friendly
46. complicated
47. turning on an axis

DOWN

1. having to do with ministers of religion
2. rude; impolite
3. dealing with events of the day
4. a crude hut or shack
5. a religious act or ceremony (1)
6. the money from some activity
7. to satisfy, as a thirst
8. to occur in large numbers
9. affecting only one side or party
16. put together in layers
17. happening by chance
18. not clear or precise
19. to give a name to
21. the will or energy to begin
23. slight or small
24. a small, bloodsucking insect
26. dazzling
27. property saved from damage
30. carefulness in what one says
32. scorn
34. to think over carefully
35. an old, crowded apartment house
38. the form of a language used only in certain places
39. clever; shrewd (14)
40. marrying while still married

Chapter Seven

Word List 19

AMENDS	GROOM	RECUPERATE
APATHY	HAMPER	ROAN
DILATORY	LOCATE	STATIONARY
DOFF	MERE	SUPERFICIAL
ECONOMICAL	NEUTRAL	TEPID
EPISODE	ORDAIN	TIC
FITFUL		

Look up the words above in your dictionary. Note that some of the words have more than one meaning. When you feel that you know *all* the meanings of *all* the words, go on to the exercise below.

EXERCISE 19A

From the four choices under each phrase or sentence, you are to mark the one that is closest in meaning to the word appearing in italics. When the same word appears more than once, you should note that it is being used in a different sense.

1. to *hamper* progress
   (a) aid (b) hinder (c) record (d) sneer at

2. a large *hamper*
   (a) bottle (b) pan (c) basket (d) closet

3. to be *dilatory* in answering
   (a) engaged (b) careful (c) slow (d) hasty

4. a *neutral* color
   (a) permanent (b) indefinite (c) strong (d) faded

5. a *neutral* observer
   (a) sharp-eyed (b) not taking sides (c) experienced (d) concealed

6. It is *ordained*.
   (a) arranged beforehand (b) blessed by a priest (c) carefully noted (d) to be feared

7. When was she *ordained*?
   (a) released from the agreement (b) made a member of the clergy (c) accepted into the service (d) awarded a degree

8. a *fitful* sleep
   (a) very short (b) healthful (c) deep (d) broken

9. to *make amends*
   (a) do emergency repairs (b) do good to make up for harm done (c) try over and over (d) start over again

10. a facial *tic*
    (a) ache (b) twitching (c) molelike blemish (d) treatment

11. a *roan* horse
    (a) untamed (b) reddish-brown sprinkled with white (c) black with white patches (d) swift

12. a feeling of *apathy*
    (a) not caring (b) not happy (c) great fear (d) extreme disgust

13. *superficial* injuries
    (a) untreated (b) slow to heal (c) extensive (d) slight

14. *mere* pennies
    (a) worn (b) rare (c) false (d) only

15. an *economical* grocer
    (a) lacking money (b) not wasteful (c) always busy (d) poorly educated

16. to *doff* one's cap
    (a) lose (b) carry (c) roll up (d) remove

17. *tepid* water
    (a) lukewarm (b) germ-free (c) cold (d) dirty

18. a startling *episode*
    (a) report (b) incident (c) picture (d) confession

19. to *recuperate* after an illness
    (a) return home (b) return to work (c) get well again (d) be taken ill again

20. The *groom* was late.

(a) person who makes deliveries (b) person who sweeps chimneys (c) man about to be married (d) man who operates a vehicle

21. to *groom* a horse
    (a) ride at a gallop (b) brush and clean (c) put a harness on (d) exhibit at a show

22. The vehicle was *stationary*.
    (a) out of date (b) moving (c) easy to operate (d) not moving

23. *located* downtown
    (a) needed (b) moved (c) hidden (d) situated

24. to *locate* someone
    (a) despise (b) find (c) need (d) join

Check your answers against the correct ones below. The answers are not in order; this is to prevent your eye catching sight of the correct ones before you have had a chance to do the exercise on your own.

10b. 16d. 5b. 22d. 12a. 20c. 4b. 21b. 15b. 9b. 1b. 24b. 11b. 13d. 7b. 23d. 17a. 18b. 6a. 2c. 14d. 19c. 8d. 3c.

Go back to your dictionary and look up again those words for which you gave incorrect answers. Only after doing this should you go on to the next exercise.

EXERCISE 19B

Each word from Word List 19 is used four times in the following sentences; one of the sentences in each group uses the word incorrectly. You are to circle the letter that precedes that sentence. Do not circle more than one letter in any one group.

1. (a) He was *ordained* a minister at the age of twenty-four. (b) She believes that the future is *ordained* by fate. (c) She *ordained* to appear, although she had been ordered to do so. (d) It seems that this nation was *ordained* to be a great power.

2. (a) The horses moved at a fast *roan* around the

field. (b) The *roan* is my horse and the chestnut mare is my sister's. (c) The *roan* mare is the best horse in the stable. (d) One horse was black and the other was *roan*.

3. (a) They sent a *mere* child to do an adult's work. (b) He is so *mere* that I don't think he can do the job alone. (c) We must rise above *mere* politics and think of the security of the nation. (d) I *merely* wanted to say that I agree with you.

4. (a) She has taken a *recuperative* and should be better soon. (b) Sleep has great *recuperative* powers. (c) He will be *recuperating* for quite a while, since his illness was quite serious. (d) The animals began to *recuperate* as soon as they got water.

5. (a) The story is told in thirty *episodes*. (b) It is not easy to *episode* one's entire life into less than 300 pages. (c) He considers his wartime experiences as a spy merely an *episode* in his life. (d) She remembers vividly certain *episodes* of her childhood in Wyoming.

6. (a) They regret treating you so unfairly and wish to make *amends*. (b) The hotel has many *amends*, including a golf course and a swimming pool. (c) First you must apologize to her, then offer to make *amends*. (d) Nothing he can do will make *amends* for his shabby treatment of you.

7. (a) He soaked his elbow in a bowl of *tepid* water. (b) The comedy act drew only a *tepid* response from the audience. (c) Oil becomes *tepid* at freezing temperatures and is difficult to pour. (d) Interest in the election was *tepid* until the last few days.

8. (a) I bought a box of *stationary* and some stamps. (b) The cat remained quite *stationary*, staring into the hole. (c) A *stationary* engine is one that is fixed in one place. (d) Prices remained *stationary* on the stock exchange yesterday.

9. (a) Traffic was *hampered* by a parade passing through the center of town. (b) The car was

hampered deep in the mud and couldn't be moved. (c) She feels that rules of grammar *hamper* free expression. (d) We packed a picnic *hamper* and left at sunrise.

10. (a) Switzerland stayed *neutral* in both world wars. (b) When the gearbox is in *neutral*, power is not being transmitted to the drive shaft. (c) The walls are painted in *neutral* shades to blend with any color scheme you choose. (d) A sprinkling of lime helps to *neutral* the acid in the soil.

11. (a) The *groom* led the horse out of the stable. (b) He is being *groomed* for a job on the board of directors. (c) Patches of *groom* grew beside the windows of the little house. (d) The *groom* dropped the ring as he was about to place it on the bride's finger.

12. (a) The new *superficial* is in charge of the entire department. (b) I read a *superficial* account of the affair in the newspapers. (c) The wound was *superficial* and healed quickly. (d) The differences between us are *superficial* and can be ignored.

13. (a) "Good morning," he said, *doffing* his hat. (b) We *doffed* the paint from the walls with razor blades. (c) He *doffed* his cape, bowing gracefully as he did so. (d) It is time they *doffed* their rose-colored glasses and saw conditions as they really are.

14. (a) They tried to hold up the work by starting late and using other *dilatory* tactics. (b) She is always eager to receive letters but is *dilatory* in answering them. (c) He was *dilatory* three mornings in a row because his alarm clock didn't go off. (d) Though *dilatory* in making plans, she is speedy when it comes to carrying them out.

15. (a) His education was *fitful* to say the least, and I don't think he ever finished a complete year. (b) A few shots were fired *fitfully* by the two armies during the night. (c) After taking a month's vacation, he felt very *fitful*. (d) They

slept *fitfully* because of the thunder.

16. (a) They decided to *locate* the new factory just outside of town. (b) I was asked to *locate* Bombay on the map of India. (c) The police have *located* the car that was stolen yesterday. (d) The office was moved to a new *locate*.

17. (a) The *tics* burrow under the skin and are very hard to remove. (b) He recovered completely from his nervous breakdown, but it left him with a *tic* under his right eye. (c) She was unable to control the *tic* which lifted the side of her mouth slightly. (d) The *tic* was so slight you could barely notice it.

18. (a) The nurse spread some *apathy* over the cut and then bandaged it. (b) Have you ever known the dull *apathy* of despair? (c) She is so *apathetic*; once she was a happy, lively girl. (d) We are concerned over the *apathy* of the voters during elections.

19. (a) Sea power is still the most *economical* form of military power. (b) She is an expert on banking and other *economical* matters. (c) He is very *economical* and manages on very little money. (d) She writes in an exact and *economical* style.

EXERCISE 19C

Rewrite each of the following sentences, replacing the italicized word or phrase with a word from Word List 19 and writing the word in the form that fits the rest of the sentence. Use each word only once. Write your answers in the spaces provided.

1. The *person who takes care of the horses* led out a *reddish-brown horse flecked with white* and walked it around the ring.

   . . . .

   . . . .

2. For a *sum that is no more than* five dollars you can buy this *large wicker basket*.

   . . . .

. . . .

3. The children are sorry for being so *slow in starting* and wish to make *up for what they know was wrong.*

. . . .

. . . .

4. His sleep was *disturbed from time to time* last night, but he continues to *get better after his illness.*

. . . .

. . . .

5. The role of the nations that remained *uncommitted to either side during the war* is an interesting *part of the story* in itself.

. . . .

. . . .

6. She was willing to *set up* her business in a slum area, but the *lack of interest* of the city officials decided her against it.

. . . .

. . . .

7. Since food and housing costs often do not stay *at their present level,* families can be *careful about how and when they spend their money* and still not have any savings.

. . . .

. . . .

8. When he *took off* his broad-brimmed hat, I noticed the *slight twitching of a muscle* at the corner of his eye.

. . . .

. . . .

9. Since the water that fell on the children was

barely *lukewarm,* I fail to see how they could have suffered even *very slight* burns.

. . . .

. . . .

10. She was one of the first women in this community to be *made a minister of the church.*

. . . .

. . . .

EXERCISE 19D

A SUPERFICIAL wound is one that does not go beneath the surface; the word comes from the Latin prefix *super-* (above) joined to the Latin *facies* (face). *Super-* can also mean "superior to" or "greater than."

Complete the sentences below by filling in the appropriate word that begins with the Latin prefix *super-.*

1. _____ speeds are those greater than the speed of sound.

2. A _____ is a person placed over others to see that they work properly.

3. A _____ effort is one that is greater than one could reasonably expect of a person.

4. A _____ is a store having a greater choice and variety of goods than does the little corner grocery.

5. Anything greater than what is needed is _____ .

6. Anything set aside as inferior or out of date has been _____ by what replaces it.

7. Something built above something else, as the part of a ship above the deck, is called the _____ .

8. Soldiers are required to salute their _____ officers.

9. A tracing can be _____ on a map
by being laid over it.

10. *Best* is the _____ form of the
adjective *good*.

EXERCISE 19E

Write out, in the spaces provided, the words
from Word List 19 for which a definition, homonym,
synonym, or antonym is given below. When you
are asked to give a root or a prefix, you should
refer back to the preceding exercise; the
information you require will be found there. Make
sure that each of your answers has the same
number of letters as there are spaces. A definition
followed by a number is a review word; the
number gives the Word List from which it is taken.

If all the words are filled in correctly, the
boxes running up and down the answer spaces will
continue the poem begun earlier.

1. a reddish-brown horse flecked with white

2. to destroy completely (17)

3. an antonym for *fervor*

4. a synonym for *hinder*

5. to recover one's health and strength

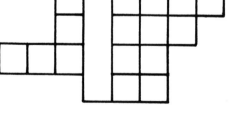

6. a sudden, sharp pain (10)

7. slightly warm

8. something done to make up for an insult or injury

9. a slight muscular spasm, especially of the face

10. a synonym for *situate*

11. an antonym for *moving*

12. an antonym for *don*

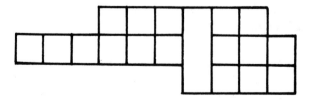

13. an antonym for *wasteful*

14. a synonym for *slow*

15. a synonym for *slight*

16. to make neat and tidy

17. to order or establish beforehand

18. a happening or incident that forms part of the main story

19. to name (18)

20. an antonym for *steady*

21. the art of using words skillfully (2)

22. not taking sides in a war or dispute

23. A Latin prefix meaning "above"

24. no more than

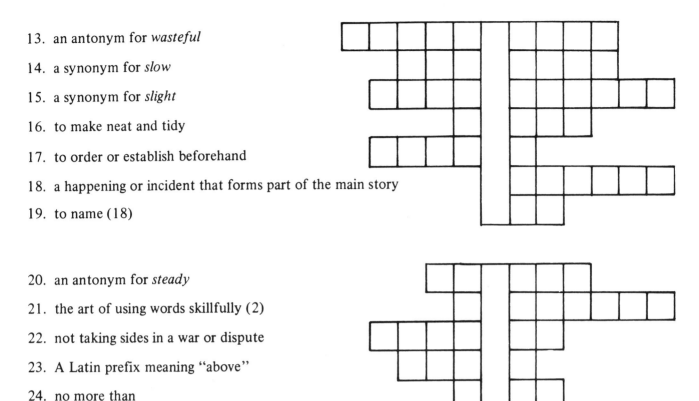

WORDLY WISE 19

Both DOFF and its antonym *don* have a rather old-fashioned flavor to them; generally speaking, these two words have been replaced by "take off" and "put on."

ECONOMICAL means "concerned with saving money" or "thrifty." *Economics* is the study of how and why the goods and services in a society are produced, distributed, and consumed.

STATIONARY (with an "a" before the "r") means "not moving." *Stationery* (with an "e" before the "r") means "writing materials." These two words are pronounced the same. Perhaps if you think of "standing still" and "letters," you will not get them confused.

A TIC is a facial spasm or twitching of a muscle. A *tick* (Word List 16) can be (a) a small bloodsucking insect, (b) a small check mark, (c) the clicking sound made by a timepiece. Don't confuse these two words.

Word List 20

ABATE	GLIB	NAUSEOUS
AGHAST	INCREDIBLE	NOMINATE
CLERGY	INIQUITOUS	PROBE
DAMASK	LOOT	STAGNANT
ERUDITE	MERGE	STATURE
FACADE	MISNOMER	UNDERTONE
FERMENT		

Look up the words above in your dictionary. Note that some of the words have more than one meaning. When you feel that you know *all* the meanings of *all* the words, go on to the exercise below.

EXERCISE 20A

From the four choices under each phrase or sentence, you are to mark the one that is closest in meaning to the word appearing in italics. When the same word appears more than once, you should note that it is being used in a different sense.

1. an *iniquitous* act
   (a) unnecessary (b) unthinking (c) wicked (d) stupid

2. an *erudite* person
   (a) ignorant (b) careless (c) well-read, knowledgeable (d) meddlesome

3. a *glib* speech
   (a) hurried (b) too long (c) smoothly spoken (d) poorly delivered

4. to put up a *facade*
   (a) false front (b) strong defense (c) sectional building (d) protective fence

5. I was *aghast*.
   (a) delighted (b) sad (c) wounded (d) horrified

6. of average *stature*
   (a) intelligence (b) weight (c) height (d) education

7. made of *damask*
   (a) woven grass (b) richly patterned, woven cloth (c) heavy, dark wood (d) carved green stone

8. to hide the *loot*
   (a) preliminary report (b) real purpose (c) stolen goods (d) final result

9. *stagnant* water
   (a) fresh (b) motionless (c) running (d) clean

10. Whom will they *nominate*?
    (a) charge with the crime (b) decide to let go (c) put in charge (d) name as a candidate

11. in a *ferment*
    (a) state of perfect bliss (b) fit of temper (c) mood of despair (d) state of agitation

12. It slowly *ferments*.
    (a) changes to alcohol (b) settles to the bottom (c) dissolves (d) goes bad

13. It will *abate*.
    (a) remain unchanged (b) grow worse (c) stop (d) become less

14. a *nauseous* smell
    (a) powerful (b) unfamiliar (c) sickening (d) appetizing

15. in an *undertone*
    (a) place of concealment (b) spirit of secrecy (c) low voice (d) strong current

16. a dark *undertone*
    (a) wicked act (b) thought that lingers in the mind (c) background color (d) purpose

17. It is a *misnomer*.
    (a) slight misunderstanding (b) situation that no one understands (c) name that does not fit (d) terrible mistake

18. to *probe* a wound
    (a) examine (b) cover (c) cause (d) stitch up

19. a government *probe*
    (a) department (b) building (c) investigation (d) law office

20. an *incredible* discovery

(a) important (b) useful (c) unbelievable (d) profitable

21. to *merge* with one another
(a) make an agreement (b) combine (c) compete (d) exchange ideas

22. a member of the *clergy*
(a) ruling body of a state (b) class of ministers, priests and rabbis (c) association of professional men and women (d) council of navy, army, and air force officers

Check your answers against the correct ones below. The answers are not in order; this is to prevent your eye catching sight of the correct ones before you have had a chance to do the exercise on your own.

10d. 16c. 5d. 22b. 12a. 20c. 4a. 21b. 15c. 9b. 1c. 11d. 13d. 7b. 17c. 18a. 6c. 2c. 14c. 19c. 8c. 3c.

Go back to your dictionary and look up again those words for which you gave incorrect answers. Only after doing this should you go on to the next exercise.

EXERCISE 20B

Each word from Word List 20 is used four times in the following sentences; one of the sentences in each group uses the word incorrectly. You are to circle the letter that precedes that sentence. Do not circle more than one letter in any one group.

1. (a) He's a *glib*-tongued fellow, but likeable for all that. (b) She *glibbed* her speech so effortlessly that I was sure he had memorized it. (c) She answered the questions *glibly*, as though bored by the whole business. (d) She's a *glib* young woman, so be careful not to let her talk.

2. (a) The cloth was pale blue, with dark blue *damasks* around the edge. (b) The best *damask* table linen was brought out for the guests. (c) The drapes are a beautiful soft *damask* color. (d) *Damask* was first made in Damascus, Syria.

3. (a) The smell is coming from that pool of *stagnant* water. (b) He needed a change; he had no desire to *stagnant* in his present job. (c) The cellar had been closed up for so long that the air in it was *stagnant* and foul. (d) The energy shortage has revived the once *stagnating* coal-mining industry.

4. (a) She *probed* me a number of questions which I refused to answer. (b) A number of space *probes* are planned for the next few months. (c) He asked some *probing* questions in an effort to get to the truth. (d) The doctor *probed* the wound, searching for metal fragments.

5. (a) The fear of war breaking out has *abated* somewhat. (b) The price was fifty dollars, but she offered an *abate* of ten percent. (c) We decided not to ask Father until his anger had *abated*. (d) The storm showed no sign of *abating*, so we decided to stay overnight with our friends.

6. (a) The Great Pyramids of Egypt were built at *incredible* cost. (b) She had a tale of *incredible* adventure to tell. (c) He looked *incredibly* at me when I told him the price. (d) The children's appetite after a day in the country is simply *incredible*.

7. (a) It is a *misnomer* to call such works of fiction "biographies." (b) They *misnomered* the star of their basketball team "Fumblefingers." (c) He found to his delight that "Mountain View" was no *misnomer* for the lodge. (d) "Vegetable," when used to describe tomatoes, is a *misnomer*.

8. (a) The grapes are pressed in this *ferment*, and the juice runs out here. (b) She has another novel *fermenting* in her brain. (c) The juices *ferment* and turn into alcohol. (d) The convention hall was in a *ferment* when the results of the voting were announced.

9. (a) If you can play the guitar, you will have no difficulty playing the *loot*. (b) The thieves

dropped their *loot* and ran when they heard the police. (c) Many of the art museums of Europe were *looted* by the Nazis during World War II. (d) The police will shoot anyone caught *looting*.

10. (a) The university will gain in *stature* by adding a medical school. (b) The people of the region are of somewhat small *stature*. (c) Her last book added considerably to her *stature* as a novelist. (d) Small pieces of *stature* dotted the gardens of the house.

11. (a) She is a political *nominate* of the governor of the state. (b) Justices of the Supreme Court are *nominated* by the president. (c) We must *nominate* a very strong candidate if we are to have a chance of winning the election. (d) It is still uncertain who will win the Republican *nomination*.

12. (a) The smell from the barrel made me feel *nauseous*. (b) A *nauseous* smell came from the ship's hold. (c) I was overcome with *nausea* and had to lie down for a while. (d) He has a smooth and oily manner that I find quite *nauseous*.

13. (a) Individual differences *merge* and become lost. (b) He was completely *merged* in his book and didn't hear me come in. (c) The two streams of traffic *merge* into one lane just ahead. (d) The government may prevent the *merger* of the two companies.

14. (a) In 1929 the *facade* of American prosperity collapsed. (b) She opened the jar of *facade* and smeared some on her cheeks. (c) The store was simply a wooden shack with an elaborate *facade*. (d) She tried to sound happy, but it was all a *facade*.

15. (a) They were *aghast* when they saw the condition the hospital was in. (b) He stared *aghast* at the blood oozing from the bullet hole. (c) The phantom horseman had an *aghast* appearance that sent shivers down our spines. (d) She was *aghast* when she saw how lax the discipline was.

16. (a) He complained that the money had been divided *iniquitously*. (b) It is *iniquitous* that such crimes go unpunished. (c) To be prevented from voting is an *iniquity* in our democratic society. (d) Bribery is doubly *iniquitous* for it corrupts both giver and taker.

17. (a) They *undertoned* so softly to each other that I couldn't hear a word. (b) There was an *undertone* of fear in his voice. (c) The light blue *undertone* seems to bring out the highlights. (d) She said something in an *undertone* to her friend.

18. (a) Members of the *clergy* travel at reduced rates. (b) He has been a *clergy*man for over fifty years. (c) We never saw him without his black coat and hat and *clergy* collar. (d) The younger sons of a nobleman had three choices: the army, the law, and the *clergy*.

19 (a) She was an *erudite* woman, but she never tries to show off her learning. (b) This is a subject of interest only to the most *erudite* of scholars. (c) He displays his *erudition* with grace and wit. (d) She asked me to *erudite* the next passage in the book.

EXERCISE 20C

Rewrite each of the following sentences, replacing the italicized word or phrase with a word from Word List 20 and writing the word in the form that fits the rest of the sentence. Use each word only once. Write your answers in the spaces provided.

1. We could detect an *underlying feeling* of worry beneath his *false appearance* of cheerfulness.

. . . .

. . . .

2. "Shrimp" is certainly an *inappropriate name* for a girl of her *height*.

. . . .

. . . .

3. The business world was in a *state of great
excitement* at the news that the two companies
were going to *combine into one company*.

. . . .

. . . .

4. All the *stolen property* has been recovered
except for some *richly patterned, woven*
tablecloths.

. . . .

. . . .

5. I was *absolutely horrified* when I heard of his
wicked and unjust treatment of you.

. . . .

. . . .

6. It is *hard to believe* that the party would
choose as its candidate for office such a
smooth-talking person.

. . . .

. . . .

7. After she had *made a thorough examination of*
the wound, the doctor promised me that the
pain would soon *grow less*.

. . . .

. . . .

8. Not all the *ministers, priests, and rabbis* are
deeply-learned people.

. . . .

. . . .

9. The water in the ditch is *stale and dirty
because it does not flow*, and that is why it has
such a *sickening* smell.

. . . .

. . . .

EXERCISE 20D

INCREDIBLE means "scarcely believable"
and is made up of the Latin prefix *in-* (discussed in
Exercise 5D) together with the root *cred* (from the
Latin *credere*, meaning "to believe") and the
adjective suffix *-ible*. This root appears in a number
of words suggesting belief or believing.

Complete the words below for which prefixes
and suffixes have been supplied by filling in the
Latin root that means "believe." Give a brief
definition for each word and check each answer in
your dictionary.

1. in _____ulous

. . . .

2. _____o

. . . .

3. _____entials

. . . .

4. dis_____it

. . . .

5. _____ence

. . . .

6. _____ible

. . . .

EXERCISE 20E

Write out, in the spaces provided, the words
from Word List 20 for which a definition,

homonym, synonym, or antonym is given below. When you are asked to give a root or a prefix, you should refer back to the preceding exercise; the information you require will be found there. Make sure that each of your answers has the same number of letters as there are spaces. A definition followed by a number is a review word; the number gives the Word List from which it is taken.

If all the words are filled in correctly, the boxes running up and down the answer spaces will continue the poem begun earlier.

1. a person who is made use of by others (8)

2. an antonym for *inarticulate*

3. to save, as from fire or shipwreck (18)

4. a Latin root meaning "believe"

5. a synonym for *sickening*

6. a false or fake front

7. a synonym for *lessen*

8. a homonym for *lute*

9. a state of great excitement

10. a synonym for *unbelievable*

11. a subdued or background color

12. a synonym for *wicked*

13. to name to an office or position

14. ministers, priests, and rabbis, as a group

15. a small, mouselike animal (13)

16. a synonym for *horrified*

17. an antonym for *separate*

18. an antonym for *flowing*

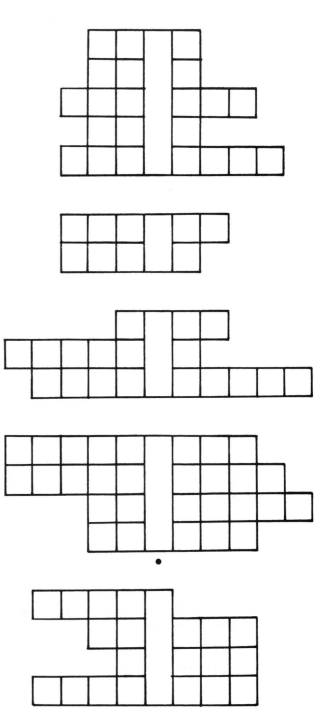

19. a synonym for *height*

20. a name that does not fit or is misapplied

21. richly patterned, woven cloth, used for table linen

22. a synonym for *investigation*

23. an antonym for *ignorant*

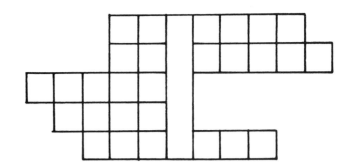

WORDLY WISE 20

When a substance such as grape juice or malt begins to FERMENT, a chemical change, brought about by yeast or bacteria, takes place which changes grape juice into wine, or malt into beer. This process is accompanied by great bubbling and giving off of gases. This action has given rise to a second meaning of *ferment:* "to seethe with excitement" or "to cause to seethe with excitement." In this second meaning (which also has a noun form), the word is easily confused with *foment*, which means "to excite or stir up trouble of some kind." *Foment* suggests a harmful activity; *ferment* suggests neither harmful nor harmless activity, but could apply to either.

INCREDIBLE means "scarcely believable." *Incredulous* means "disbelieving." If your story is *incredible*, your listeners will be *incredulous*.

NAUSEOUS means "causing a feeling of sickness." *Nauseated* means "feeling sick." Thus, if you smell something *nauseous*, you will feel *nauseated*. Neither of these words ought to be used in place of the other.

The verb form of the adjective STAGNANT is *stagnate*. Water that *stagnates* becomes *stagnant*.

Word List 21

ADROIT	DESOLATE	RABBLE
AMBIGUOUS	DISCOMFITED	REPRIEVE
AWE	EPITAPH	SANCTUARY
COLOSSAL	EXECUTE	STABLE
CONCUR	KINDLE	SWATHE
CORROBORATE	LURID	TRITE

Look up the words above in your dictionary. Note that some of the words have more than one meaning. When you feel that you know *all* the meanings of *all* the words, go on to the next exercise.

EXERCISE 21A

From the four choices under each phrase or sentence, you are to mark the one that is closest in meaning to the word appearing in italics. When the same word appears more than once, you should note that it is being used in a different sense.

1. a feeling of *awe*
(a) despair (b) tiredness (c) wonder (d) hope

2. to *execute* a person
(a) capture after a chase (b) search for (c) lawfully put to death (d) send to prison

3. to *execute* the plan
(a) put into effect (b) draw up (c) vote against (d) drop

4. The *stable* needs repairing.
(a) covered bridge (b) building where horses are housed (c) center part of a wooden cart wheel (d) covered porch on a house

5. a *stable* influence
(a) unsettling (b) unsavory (c) steadying (d) powerful

6. to *swathe* a wound
(a) examine by probing into (b) bind with a cloth (c) neglect (d) leave exposed to the air

7. a *colossal* statue
(a) enormous (b) very old (c) valuable (d) stone

8. We read the *epitaph*.
   (a) final passage of a book (b) inscription on a tombstone (c) message written in code (d) short, witty saying

9. granted a *reprieve*
   (a) new trial (b) private meeting with a head of state (c) postponement of a death sentence (d) license to produce goods

10. to *corroborate* the story
    (a) confirm (b) listen to (c) agree to publish (d) cover up

11. an *ambiguous* remark
    (a) short and witty (b) having more than one meaning (c) amusing in an unkind way (d) long, clumsy, and involved

12. a *trite* remark
    (a) whispered (b) clever (c) carefully thought out (d) overused

13. to feel *discomfited*
    (a) hungry (b) tired (c) embarrassed (d) sore

14. the *lurid* details
    (a) shocking (b) boring (c) unimportant (d) carefully detailed

15. a *lurid* glow
    (a) warm and comforting (b) hazy red (c) dim (d) mysterious

16. to set up a *sanctuary*
    (a) system of government (b) place of safety (c) group to look into complaints (d) charitable organization

17. to be forced to *concur*
    (a) change (b) obey (c) surrender (d) agree

18. Did the events *concur?*
    (a) prove the theory (b) happen together (c) fail to take place (d) disprove the theory

19. to look over the *rabble*
    (a) list of names (b) noisy crowd of people (c) letter signed by many people (d) broken stone and brick

20. a *desolate* spot

(a) densely populated (b) lonely (c) attractive (d) known to few people

21. She was *desolate*.
    (a) very unattractive (b) overjoyed (c) very attractive (d) very unhappy

22. to *kindle* interest in a cause
    (a) take a good deal of (b) put an end to (c) have little (d) arouse

23. *adroitly* take place
    (a) secretly (b) skillfully (c) clumsily (d) partially

Check your answers against the correct ones below. The answers are not in order; this is to prevent your eye catching sight of the correct ones before you have had a chance to do the exercise on your own.

10a. 16b. 5c. 12d. 20b. 4b. 21d. 15b. 9c. 1c. 11b. 13c. 7a. 17d. 18b. 6b. 2c. 14a. 19b. 8b. 3a. 22d. 23b.

Go back to your dictionary and look up again those words for which you gave incorrect answers. Only after doing this should you go on to the next exercise.

EXERCISE 21B

Each word from Word List 21 is used four times in the sentences below; one of the sentences in each group uses the word incorrectly. You are to circle the letter that precedes that sentence. Do not circle more than one letter in any one group.

1. (a) He was *ambiguous* which road to take when he came to the fork. (b) The *ambiguity* of her position seems not to bother her. (c) She never answers directly, always *ambiguously*. (d) The messages received by the thieves from their leader were always expressed *ambiguously*.

2. (a) We threw lots of *kindle* on the fire to get it started. (b) He *kindled* hopes in their breasts that he was unable to fulfill. (c) I'll *kindle* the fire while you gather more firewood. (d) Her imagination was *kindled* by the stories she read.

3. (a) It was an easy task for Mark Antony to turn the *rabble* against Brutus. (b) Some called him a great orator, while others called him a

rabble-rouser. (c) The stunning defeat turned the fleeing army into a confused *rabble*. (d) She *rabbled* quickly through her papers to see if she could find the missing deed.

4. (a) The *sanctuary* was a hidden place which only members could enter. (b) The island is being made into a wildlife *sanctuary*. (c) Many people who fled from Nazi Germany found *sanctuary* in this country. (d) He has a *sanctuary* manner that annoys people.

5. (a) The mower cut a wide *swathe* through the cornfield. (b) We *swathed* our legs in sacking as added protection against the cold. (c) The workmen removed the cotton *swathes* that had been wrapped around the statue. (d) His head was *swathed* in a bright red turban.

6. (a) She looked quite *discomfited* when asked what she wanted. (c) Her eyes were *discomfited* from the acid fumes. (c) He tripped over his shoelaces and got to his feet looking quite *discomfited*. (d) The robbers, greatly *discomfited* at seeing the police, raised their arms.

7. (a) His *adroit* replies to the hecklers in the crowd caused great amusement. (b) She drew an *adroit*-angled triangle on the blackboard. (c) Her *adroitness* in debate brought her lots of admirers. (d) He *adroitly* slipped the headwaiter a five-dollar bill.

8. (a) A *colossal* statue stood at the entrance to the harbor. (b) A stone *colossal* guarded the entrance to the tomb. (c) Attempting to steal the crown jewels from the Tower of London took *colossal* nerve. (d) We found that we had made a *colossal* blunder.

9. (a) The novel has fifteen chapters, not counting a five-page *epitaph*. (b) The *epitaph* was barely legible, so worn was the tombstone. (c) Here was a woman who did her best; let that be her *epitaph*. (d) The *epitaph* on the poet's grave consisted of eight lines from his best-loved poem.

10. (a) She walked down the deserted main street, which looked *desolate* in the pouring rain. (b) The *desolate* cries of the children almost broke my heart. (c) She likes to go away to a cabin she has in the most *desolate* part of Maine. (d) When they were at a safe distance, they *desolated* the explosive charge and blew up the building.

11. (a) He was *reprieved* just minutes before being strapped into the electric chair. (b) Only the state governor can grant a *reprieve* to the condemned person. (c) Unless there is an eleventh hour *reprieve*, the subways will stop running tomorrow. (d) They tried to *reprieve* the lost oar, but it was swept away by the current.

12. (a) "It's a small world," he said *tritely*. (b) We left before he could *trite* any more of his stupid remarks. (c) She was full of *trite* sayings. (d) "Why Homework Should Be Abolished" is a *trite* subject for an essay.

13. (a) A look of *awe* came into the girls' eyes when they were introduced to their favorite author. (b) The brooch, made out of a piece of *awe*, had been polished until it shone like gold. (c) The Grand Canyon is an *awe*-inspiring sight. (d) They refused to be *awed* by their magnificent surroundings.

14. (a) He *executed* the dance steps nimbly and precisely. (b) The prisoner was led before the firing squad, blindfolded, and *executed*. (c) The soldiers marched exactly fifteen paces, then *executed* to the left. (d) The finished piece of sculpture will be *executed* in bronze.

15. (a) The witch *lurid* Hansel and Gretel to her house. (b) There were some paperback thrillers at the newsstand with the usual *lurid* titles. (c) The flames threw a *lurid* glow on the firefighters struggling to put out the fire. (d) The newspapers were full of *lurid* details of the scandal.

16. (a) Two fins sticking out of the sides help to

stable the ship. (b) We *stabled* the horses in the barn for the night. (c) The trouble with the country is that it lacks a *stable* government. (d) It is no use locking the *stable* door after the horse has bolted.

17. (a) The two authors *corroborated* with each other in the writing of the book. (b) The police asked me if I could *corroborate* his story. (c) She hopes this new discovery will provide *corroboration* for her theory. (d) All the tests we have conducted *corroborate* our earlier findings.

18. (a) All present *concurred* in the decision. (b) Do you *concur* with the opinions expressed? (c) The Normans sailed from their homes in 1066 to *concur* England. (d) Several events must *concur* to bring about such an unusual result.

EXERCISE 21C

Rewrite each of the sentences below, replacing the italicized word or phrase with a word from Word List 21 and writing the word in the form that fits the rest of the sentence. Use each word only once. Write your answers in the spaces provided.

1. The prisoner will be *put to death as ordered by law* unless the governor grants a *delay in the carrying out of the sentence.*

    . . . .

    . . . .

2. When the king saw the *noisy crowds of people* storming his palace, a look of *fear, mixed with respect and wonder,* crossed his face.

    . . . .

    . . . .

3. She tried to *stir up* the interest of her readers by giving them a *shocking and sensational* account of the tragedy.

    . . . .

    . . . .

4. He looked quite *ill at ease* when l asked him if he could *confirm the truth of* the story, and his answer was deliberately *expressed so that it could be understood several ways.*

    . . . .

    . . . .

5. The children who were on the run found *a place of safety* in the *building where the horses were housed.*

    . . . .

    . . . .

6. I *agree* with your view that building the hotel in such a *lonely and deserted* spot was a *huge* blunder.

    . . . .

    . . . .

7. The *inscription on the tombstone* consisted of a few *dull and commonplace* verses.

    . . . .

    . . . .

8. With quick, *very skillful* movements, the nurse proceeded to *completely cover* his foot in bandages.

    . . . .

    . . . .

EXERCISE 21D

An EPITAPH is an inscription upon a tombstone; the word comes from the Greek prefix *epi-* (upon) plus the Greek *taphos* (a tomb).

Here are eight more Greek words:

hemera	(day)
legein	(to speak)
demos	(the people)
glotta	(tongue)
tithenal	(to put)
dermis	(skin)
stellein	(to send)
temnein	(to cut)

Combining roots from the above words with the Greek prefix *epi-*, construct words to match the following definitions. Check each answer in your dictionary for accuracy and spelling.

1. lasting only a day; short-lived

   . . . .

2. a disease that quickly spreads and attacks many people

   . . . .

3. the outermost layer of the skin

   . . . .

4. the thin piece of tissue that covers the windpipe during swallowing

   . . . .

5. a final speech to the audience that concludes a play

   . . . .

6. a letter

   . . . .

7. a word or phrase that describes a person or thing by naming some quality or feature

   . . . .

8. a part or thing that is typical of the whole.

   . . . .

EXERCISE 21E

Write out, in the spaces provided, the words from Word List 21 for which a definition, homonym, synonym, or antonym is given on the next page. When you are asked to give a root or a prefix, you should refer back to the preceding exercise; the information you require will be found there. Make sure that each of your answers has the same number of letters as there are spaces. A definition followed by a number is a review word; the number gives the Word List from which it is taken.

If all the words are filled in correctly, the boxes running up and down the answer spaces will continue the poem begun earlier.

1. respect mixed with fear and wonder

2. to wrap or cover

3. ministers, priests, and rabbis (20)

4. an inscription on a tombstone

5. filled with horror (20)

6. a synonym for *mob*

7. a holy place or a place used for shelter

8. indifference; lack of interest (19)

9. an antonym for *original*

10. a delay in carrying out a sentence of death

11. an antonym for *clumsy*

12. genuine; not fake (12)

13. a Greek prefix meaning "upon"

14. a synonym for *forlorn*

15. an antonym for *shaky*

16. glowing a hazy red

17. to arouse

18. a synonym for *confirm*

19. an antonym for *disagree*

20. to put into effect

21. unclear because it could be understood in more than one sense

22. an antonym for *tiny*

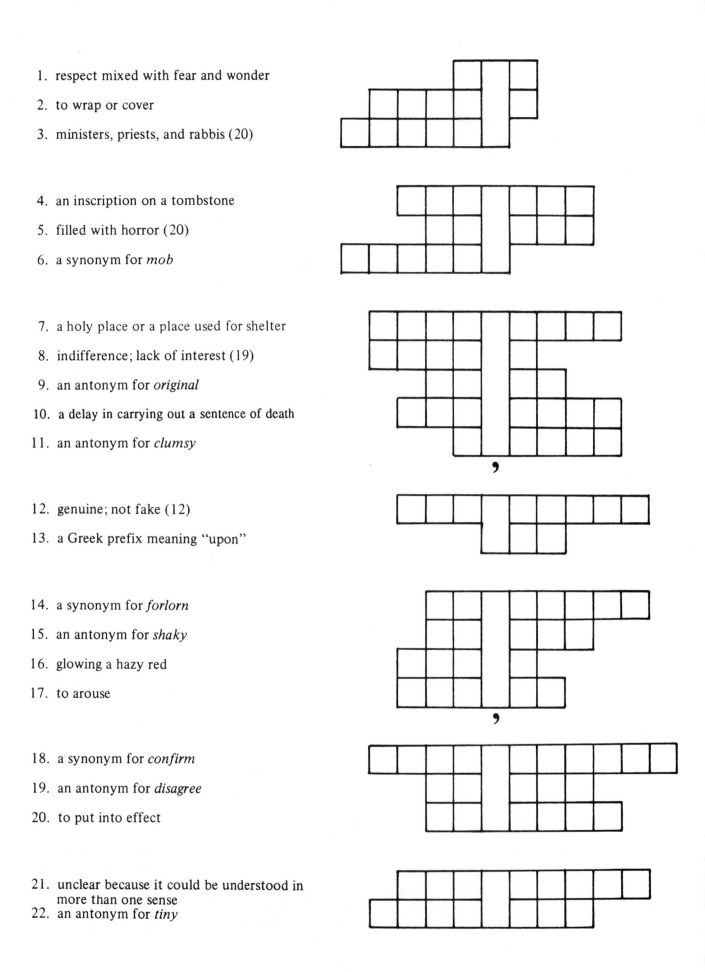

WORDLY WISE 21

ADROIT, meaning "skillful" and pronounced *a-DROYT*, comes from the French *a droit* (to the right). A word opposite in meaning is *gauche* (pronounced *goash*) that comes from the French word for *left*. *Gauche* generally refers to a lack of skill in handling social situations, an awkwardness.

A remark may be deliberately AMBIGUOUS if the speaker's intention is to puzzle or confuse his listeners. Sometimes the ambiguity is unintentional and due to carelessness, as in the sentence, "Alice told Mary that she couldn't come to the party." It is unclear whether "she" refers to Alice or to Mary.

One of the Seven Wonders of the World in ancient times was the Colossus of Rhodes, a bronze statue of Apollo over 100 feet high that dominated the harbor of Rhodes, a city on the Aegean island of Rhodes. Shakespeare's Cassius, speaking of Julius Caesar, says:

> Why, man, he doth bestride the narrow world
> Like a Colossus, and we petty men
> Walk under his huge legs. . .

From the Colossus of Rhodes has come our word COLOSSAL for anything huge or gigantic.

SWATHE is a verb and means "to wrap or bind with cloth or bandages"; it is also a noun and means "a wrapping or bandage." *Swath* (without the final *e*) is a noun and means "a strip or band (as a grass or wheat) cut with a scythe or other mowing machine." Neither of these words can be used in place of the other.

ACROSS

1. to show to be true
5. feeling great horror
10. stale and commonplace
11. easy to see or understand (18)
12. confused and embarrassed
14. to name as a candidate
15. on the surface
18. a grayish red or rose color
21. to make neat and tidy
23. clever; skillful
24. an incident or event
25. a state of great agitation
27. the height of a person
30. respect, mixed with wonder and fear
31. to show where something is
32. dejected; unhappy
35. not flowing; sluggish
39. a building for horses
40. not wasteful of time or money
42. joining neither side
44. stolen goods
45. an inscription on a tombstone
47. slightly warm
49. wicked and evil
50. a delay or postponement
53. a noisy crowd; a mob
54. causing one to feel sick
55. well-read; scholarly
56. a lack of interest

DOWN

1. enormous; gigantic
2. to get well again
3. to order; to make happen
4. an uncontrollable facial twitch
6. speaking smoothly and easily
7. something done to make up for an injury
8. slow or late in doing things
9. nothing more than; only
10. a sudden, sharp pain (10)
13. a false front
16. not regular or steady
17. to stir or shake up (2)
18. to take off; to remove
19. to combine or come together
20. to catch fire
22. a name that does not fit
24. to put to death
26. a steep, flat-topped hill (15)
27. to wrap with cloth
28. reddish-brown sprinkled with white
29. not moving
33. hard to believe
34. to become less; drop back
35. a place of safety
36. a low tone of voice
37. having two or more meanings; unclear
38. a large, covered basket
41. to agree with an opinion
43. lit up in a frightening way
46. ministers, priests, rabbis, as a group
48. a thorough investigation
51. to prepare for publication (15)
52. a ring of flowers worn around the neck (12)

Chapter Eight

Word List 22

BELLOW	ENDEAVOR	MENTOR
CHARLATAN	FICTITIOUS	RUMMAGE
COMMANDEER	GAVEL	SHODDY
CONCLUDE	INDEFATIGABLE	TACITURN
DEVOUR	INLET	TACT
EARMARK		

Look up the words above in your dictionary. Note that some of the words have more than one meaning. When you feel that you know *all* the meanings of *all* the words, go on to the exercises below.

EXERCISE 22A

From the four choices under each phrase or sentence, you are to mark the one that is closest in meaning to the word appearing in italics. When the same word appears more than once, you should note that it is being used in a different sense.

1. a narrow *inlet*
   (a) crack in the earth (b) slit in a castle wall (c) narrow channel or passage of water (d) pipe used for carrying water

2. *shoddy* material
   (a) that easily catches fire (b) poorly made (c) expensive (d) loosely woven

3. He is a *charlatan*.
   (a) qualified medical doctor (b) person who is always hopeful (c) person who is always gloomy (d) person who pretends to have a skill.

4. a trusted *mentor*
   (a) guard (b) employee (c) teacher (d) business associate

5. to *devour* the turkey
   (a) divide equally (b) eat greedily (c) remove the feathers from (d) clean out the insides of

6. to *devour* a book
   (a) sell cheaply (b) review fully (c) write quickly (d) read eagerly

7. a *fictitious* story
   (a) plausible (b) unlikely (c) true (d) made up

8. to *commandeer* the horses
   (a) sell (b) seize (c) purchase (d) train

9. a *taciturn* person
   (a) silent (b) weak (c) wise (d) generous

10. to *conclude* the matter
    (a) end (b) reopen (c) consider (d) discuss

11. to *conclude* an agreement
    (a) quarrel over (b) arrange (c) rewrite (d) oppose

12. to *conclude* that one was right
    (a) decide (b) insist (c) be forced to admit (d) be unconvinced

13. to *rummage* through the room
    (a) look directly (b) grope blindly (c) walk slowly (d) search thoroughly

14. a *rummage* sale
    (a) farm produce (b) livestock (c) odds and ends (d) going out of business

15. to have *tact*
    (a) skill with one's hands (b) skill in dealing with people (c) great intelligence (d) ability to stick to something

16. to *endeavor* to win
    (a) hope (b) expect (c) try (d) need

17. to pound the *gavel*
    (a) wooden hammer used to bring a meeting to order (b) dough used to make bread (c) block on which metal is worked (d) part that is bent out of shape

18. Don't *bellow!*
    (a) misbehave (b) roar (c) whisper (d) complain

19. *earmarked* for her own use

(a) ordered (b) purchased (c) needed (d) set aside

20. an *indefatigable* swimmer

(a) untiring (b) expert (c) graceful (d) fast

Check your answers against the correct ones below. The answers are not in order; this is to prevent your eye catching sight of the correct ones before you have had a chance to do the exercise on your own.

10a. 16c. 5b. 12a. 4c. 15b. 9a. 1c. 11b. 3d. 13d. 7d. 17a. 18b. 6d. 2b. 14c. 19d. 8b. 20a.

Go back to your dictionary and look up again those words for which you gave incorrect answers. Only after doing this should you go on to the next exercise.

EXERCISE 22B

Each word from Word List 22 is used four times in the sentences below; one of the sentences in each group uses the word incorrectly. You are to circle the letter that precedes that sentence. Do not circle more than one letter in any one group.

1. (a) The bull let out a loud *bellow* when the farmer hit it. (b) Pump hard on the *bellow* to get the fire started. (c) The captain stood on the bridge *bellowing* out orders. (d) The cannons *bellowed,* and sheets of flame and clouds of smoke came from their mouths.

2. (a) He lost the *tact* of his speech when his papers fell on the floor. (b) She can be very *tactless* at times. (c) The matter will have to be handled with great *tact*. (d) "I think you're both right," she said *tactfully*.

3. (a) Don't waste your money on *charlatans* and their fake cures. (b) Beware of those people with their *charlatan* tricks. (c) The industry is being taken over by rogues and *charlatans*. (d) It was to keep out *charlatans* that the first medical societies were formed.

4. (a) The pages of the book were *earmarked* from many years of use. (b) The cattle are *earmarked* before being allowed out to graze.

(c) These funds have been *earmarked* for the new dormitory. (d) This book has all the *earmarks* of a bestseller.

5. (a) Their *endeavors* to bring about a settlement were unsuccessful. (b) I *endeavored* to explain what was wrong with the plan. (c) We *endeavor* to please, but we are not always successful. (d) You are *endeavored* to appear in court tomorrow morning.

6. (a) I *concluded* that we were in serious trouble. (b) The concert was brought to a rousing *conclude* with three Sousa marches. (c) The two countries have *concluded* an agreement to exchange students. (d) She *concluded* her reading with a selection of Tennyson's poetry.

7. (a) The chairman of the meeting pounded with his *gavel* in an attempt to restore order. (b) The *gavel* was placed on the bench in front of the judge. (c) One teenager held the post in place while the other pounded it into the ground with her *gavel*. (d) When the auctioneer brings his *gavel* down for the third time, the item is sold.

8. (a) She's very interested in astronomy and *devours* any books on the subject that she can find. (b) He *devoured* everything on his plate. (c) The acid *devours* into the unprotected parts of the metal. (d) The fire spread, *devouring* everything in its path.

9. (a) The water is too *shoddy* to be drunk. (b) The blankets were made out of the cheapest kind of *shoddy*. (c) The children were very *shoddily* dressed. (d) He treated her in a very *shoddy* manner.

10. (a) The children become *indefatigable* very quickly and have to rest. (b) The boys are *indefatigable* in their efforts to finish the tree house. (c) A good hunter must have *indefatigable* patience. (d) They work *indefatigably* throughout the night.

11. (a) We crossed the *inlet* in rowboats. (b) The table was of oak *inlet* with walnut. (c) Air enters through this *inlet* and leaves through the outlet on the other side. (d) The coast is irregular with hundreds of little *inlets* running into it.

12. (a) The story she gave was obviously *fictitious*. (b) She was being *fictitious* when she said she was tired and thirsty. (c) He gave a *fictitious* name to the man at the door. (d) Although this is a *fictitious* account of Amelia Earhart's life, it is based on fact.

13. (a) When she succeeded to the throne, the young queen no longer heeded the wise counsel of her *mentor*. (b) For over forty years she was my friend and *mentor*. (c) I asked him to *mentor* the students on the origins of the Industrial Revolution. (d) Although she did not usually take students, he persuaded her to become his *mentor*.

14. (a) He *rummaged* through the piles of books looking for the one he wanted. (b) The children were playing in the little *rummage* at the back of the inn. (c) The church is holding a *rummage* sale on Saturday. (d) She waited outside while her husband *rummaged* the store in search of antiques.

15. (a) The *commandeer* of the troops gave the order to charge. (b) The soldiers crossed the river in *commandeered* boats. (c) Soldiers went from house to house *commandeering* blankets and bedding. (d) The young captain *commandeered* all the rooms in the inn for his men.

16. (a) He was a gaunt, thin-lipped, *taciturn* man. (b) She sat *taciturnly* throughout the meeting and left without a word. (c) We made a *taciturn* agreement to help each other. (d) His *taciturnity* may be due to his having nothing to say.

EXERCISE 22C

Rewrite each of the following sentences, re-placing the italicized word or phrase with a word from Word List 22 and writing the word in the form that fits the rest of the sentence. Use each word only once. Write your answers in the spaces provided.

1. The judge *made an attempt* to restore order by pounding on the bench with her *small, wooden mallet.*

   . . . .

   . . . .

2. "You are a *person who claims to have knowledge he does not possess!*" he *shouted in a loud and angry voice.*

   . . . .

   . . . .

3. The general *reached the decision* that it would be necessary to *take over, by the use of force if necessary*, all the cars and trucks in the town.

   . . . .

   . . . .

4. The only thing left over from the *odds and ends that were on* sale was a *cheap and poorly-made* sweater.

   . . . .

   . . . .

5. Aristotle was the *wise and trusted adviser* of Alexander the Great.

   . . . .

   . . . .

6. The *narrow strip of water that runs in from the sea* can be crossed at low tide.

. . . .

. . . .

7. The job is one requiring great *skill in dealing sympathetically with people.*

. . . .

. . . .

8. The old men and women are *not much given to talking* and just sit quietly by themselves.

. . . .

. . . .

9. Paul Bunyan, the *tireless* lumberjack, is of course an *imaginary and not a real* character.

. . . .

. . . .

10. The children *quickly and greedily ate* the cake that had been *set aside* for the church bazaar.

. . . .

. . . .

QUIXOTIC

definition . . . .

origin . . . .

. . . .

. . . .

. . . .

MALAPROPISM

definition . . . .

origin . . . .

. . . .

. . . .

BOYCOTT

definition . . . .

origin . . . .

. . . .

EXERCISE 22D

In Homer's great epic poem, the **Odyssey**, young Telemachus, the son of Odysseus, sets out in search of information about his father, who has been absent from home for nearly twenty years. Telemachus is accompanied in his voyage by Athene, the goddess of wisdom, in the form of Mentor, one of his father's friends. Our word MENTOR, for a wise and trusted adviser, comes from the name of Telemachus' companion.

The following words are derived from the names of actual or fictitious persons. Give a brief definition of each and follow this with a brief account of how the person's name in each case came into the language. Use a dictionary or other reference work giving word origins to track down the information you need.

EXERCISE 22E

Write out, in the spaces provided, the words from Word List 22 for which a definition, homonym, synonym, or antonym is given on the next page. When you are asked to give a root or a prefix, you should refer back to the preceding exercise; the information you require will be found there. Make sure that each of your answers has the same number of letters as there are spaces. A definition followed by a number is a review word; the number gives the Word List from which it is taken.

If all the words are filled in correctly, the boxes running up and down the answer spaces will continue the poem begun earlier.

128

1. an awareness of the right thing to say or do

2. a synonym for *roar*

3. huge, gigantic (21)

4. an antonym for *start*

5. a synonym for *quack*

6. a false front (20)

7. to seize, especially for military use

8. a wise and trusted adviser

9. barely warm (19)

10. to look into very closely (20)

11. an antonym for *actual*

12. a wooden hammer used by judges for maintaining order

13. a synonym for *try*

14. made to feel ill at ease (21)

15. a synonym for *tawdry*

16. steady and firm (21)

17. an antonym for *talkative*

18. to eat hungrily and quickly

19. a narrow section of sea running into the land

20. sudden, sharp, and irregular (18)

21. to set aside for a special purpose

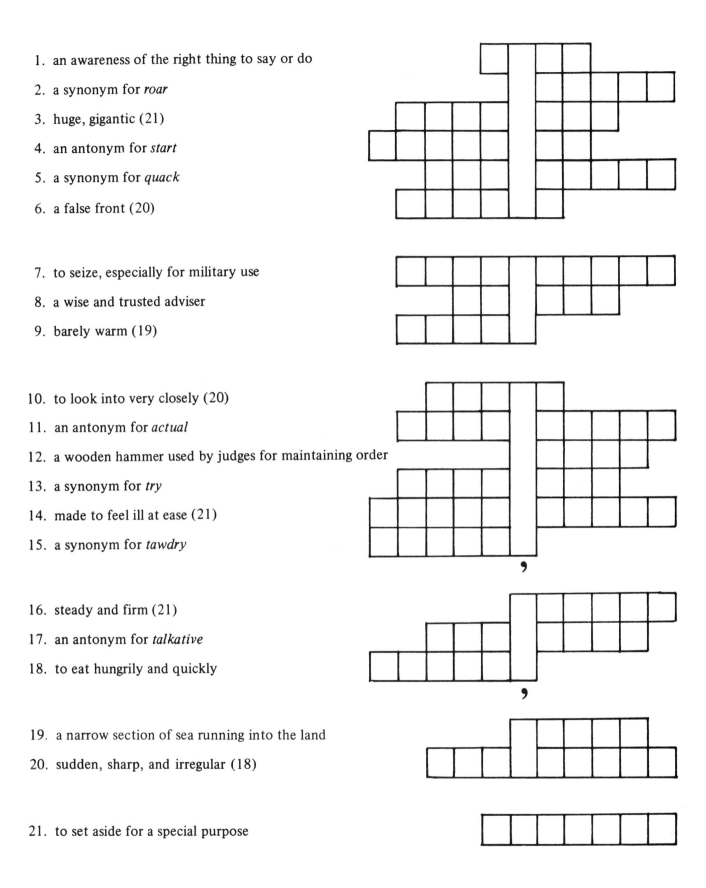

129

22. deeply absorbed or interested (14)

23. to express sorrow or regret (18)

24. currently in the news (16)

25. to search thoroughly

26. something given as a sign of affection (17)

WORDLY WISE 22

CHARLATAN, pronounced *SHAR-la-tun*, is a French word which has been incorporated into English. The French word is derived from the Latin word *ceretanus*, meaning literally, "an inhabitant of Cerreto," a town in Italy. This town was famous in story and legend for its quacks and imposters, hence the meaning of our present-day word *charlatan*.

The word EARMARK, meaning "a distinguishing characteristic," is derived from the custom of marking the ears of domestic animals for the purpose of identifying the owner, should the animal be lost or stolen.

Word List 23

ABYSMAL	DISFIGURED	PROPOSE
ARDOR	EDIBLE	RANCID
CADET	ERASE	REPRISAL
CURB	FESTIVE	SHOAL
DENOUNCE	FORESHADOW	VELOCITY
DEVOTED	INDOMITABLE	

Look up the words above in your dictionary. Note that some of the words have more than one meaning. When you feel that you know *all* the meanings of *all* the words, go on to the exercise below.

EXERCISE 23A

From the four choices under each phrase or sentence, you are to mark the one that is closest in meaning to the word appearing in italics. When the same word appears more than once, you should note that it is being used in a different sense.

1. *abysmal* poverty
(a) undeserved (b) temporary (c) deserved (d) immeasurable

2. This was a *reprisal.*
(a) gesture of goodwill (b) gesture of defiance (c) act of retaliation (d) act of war

3. The butter is *rancid.*
(a) spoiled (b) melted (c) fresh (d) burnt

4. to *denounce* the king
(a) beg a favor of (b) support secretly (c) remove from the throne (d) speak out against

5. She spoke with *ardor.*
(a) gentleness (b) enthusiasm (c) anger (d) lack of conviction

6. a *festive* occasion
(a) sad (b) gay (c) special (d) formal

7. to *propose* a plan
(a) suggest (b) examine carefully (c) keep secret (d) vote down

8. He *proposed* last night.
(a) left (b) made an offer of marriage (c) had his application turned down (d) returned

9. a *devoted* follower
(a) loyal (b) disappointed (c) young (d) recent

10. *indomitable* courage
(a) futile (b) unyielding (c) foolhardy (d) unexpected

11. a young *cadet*

(a) visitor from a foreign country (b) person learning a trade (c) student in a military college (d) person training for the priesthood

12. to reduce the *velocity*
    (a) temperature (b) speed (c) price (d) size

13. to *erase* an error
    (a) point out (b) rub out (c) make (d) try not to make

14. *edible* nuts
    (a) poisonous (b) dried out (c) unripe (d) eatable

15. to *foreshadow* something
    (a) avoid (b) try to prevent (c) indicate beforehand (d) follow

16. to follow the *shoal*
    (a) herd of deer (b) school of fish (c) dried-up riverbed (d) pack of hunting dogs

17. Be careful of *shoals*.
    (a) sudden turns (b) rocks (c) shallow places (d) accidents

18. to *curb* one's strength
    (a) measure (b) hold in check (c) increase (d) be surprised by

19. to hit the *curb*
    (a) stone edging on a street (b) mongrel dog (c) submerged rock (d) mass of floating ice

20. a *disfigured* face
    (a) showing great rage (b) crudely drawn (c) marked by an injury (d) drawn in a distorted manner

Check your answers against the correct ones below. The answers are not in order; this is to prevent your eye catching sight of the correct ones before you have had a chance to do the exercise on your own.

10b. 16b. 5b. 12b. 20c. 4d. 15c. 9a. 1d. 11c. 13b. 7a. 17c. 18b. 6b. 2c. 14d. 19a. 8b. 3a.

Go back to your dictionary and look up again those words for which you gave incorrect answers. Only after doing this should you go on to the next exercise.

EXERCISE 23B

Each word from Word List 23 is used four times in the sentences below; one of the sentences in each group uses the word incorrectly. You are to circle the letter that precedes that sentence. Do not circle more than one letter in any one group.

1. (a) She wrote an angry *denounce* of conditions in the slums. (b) His invention was *denounced* as a fraud. (c) The country has *denounced* its treaty with France. (d) The plotters against the queen were *denounced* by their former friends.

2. (a) Thirty days in the city jail will cool their *ardor*. (b) The *ardor* in his voice melted her cold heart. (c) He cursed the *ardor* of the rocks as he tried unsuccessfully to break them. (d) She loved her country with all the *ardor* of a newly-arrived immigrant.

3. (a) She *disfigured* the cost down to thirty dollars. (b) The scenery along the highway is *disfigured* by billboards. (c) The scar that *disfigured* his face was concealed through surgery. (d) The painting has been *disfigured* with a black streak of paint.

4. (a) This bacon tastes *rancid*. (b) He looked *rancidly* at his enemy. (c) Butter goes *rancid* very quickly if not kept in the icebox. (d) The air in the basement had a sour, *rancid* smell.

5. (a) The facts are *indomitable* and cannot be disputed. (b) With *indomitable* courage they fought off the attackers. (c) Under the *indomitable* leadership of Winston Churchill, Britain fought back against Hitler. (d) She has an *indomitable* will.

6. (a) Wind *velocities* of up to eighty m.p.h. were recorded yesterday. (b) To solve the problem you have to know the direction and *velocity*

of both ships. (c) She spoke with such *velocity* that it was a strain to catch her words. (d) A rocket must reach a *velocity* of seven miles per second to escape the earth's gravity.

7. (a) She was his *devoted* friend for many years. (b) After passing the resolution, they had second thoughts and *devoted* it. (c) Her servants were *devoted* to her. (d) He *devoted* five years to writing this book.

8. (a) Hitler's occupation of Czechoslovakia *foreshadowed* the Second World War. (b) She could tell by the *foreshadows* that it was getting late. (c) The discontent expressed by the people could *foreshadow* worse troubles later. (d) The little workshop of Henry Ford *foreshadowed* the gigantic automobile industry of today.

9. (a) The training ship had fifty *cadets* aboard. (b) He was willing to *cadet* for a year to see if he liked it. (c) His mother showed me a picture of him as an aviation *cadet*. (d) Senior *cadets* in military school are responsible for discipline.

10. (a) He failed *abysmally* in all his subjects. (b) The gash was so *abysmal* that it needed twelve stitches. (c) "I'm an *abysmal* failure," she said gloomily. (d) Her book deals with the *abysmal* living conditions of the poor.

11. (a) He gets excited very easily and needs to develop some *curb*. (b) Use the *curb* to control the horse. (c) The car mounted the *curb* and crashed into a tree. (d) The impertinent girl was told to *curb* her tongue.

12. (a) Let us try to *propose* our differences and work together. (b) She has been waiting for over a year for her boyfriend to *propose*. (c) The guests *proposed* a toast to the honored speaker. (d) What do you *propose* to do about the problem?

13. (a) The errors had been neatly *erased*. (b) Only time can *erase* the bitter memory of that night. (c) The city should *erase* that hole in

the road. (d) How I wish we could *erase* the mistakes of the past.

14. (a) The bombing of our headquarters was a *reprisal* for our attack. (b) The military commander will take *reprisals* if any soldiers under his command are attacked. (c) Remind me to give him a severe *reprisal* for disobeying orders. (d) The outlaws threatened to kill six townspeople as a *reprisal* if their leader were hanged.

15. (a) A *festive* group of peasants joined the party. (b) A *festive* air surrounded the preparations for Christmas. (c) Fly the flag on all *festive* occasions. (d) The *festives* began with a fireworks display.

16. (a) The fish swim between the sandy *shoals*. (b) The fish swim in *shoals* and are easily netted. (c) They *shoaled* up the side of the tunnel with stout poles. (d) The boat almost touched bottom as it passed over the *shoal*.

17. (a) Many vegetables are *edible* whether cooked or raw. (b) Some kinds of seaweed are *edible*. (c) The water is dirty, but it is quite *edible*. (d) They brought cold meats and other *edibles* with them.

EXERCISE 23C

Rewrite each of the sentences below, replacing the italicized word or phrase with a word from Word List 23 and writing the word in the form that fits the rest of the sentence. Use each word only once. Write your answers in the spaces provided.

1. The first manned space flights *are a sign of* future trips to the planets and beyond, in rockets travelling at incredible *speeds*.

   . . . .

   . . . .

2. The colonel *made the suggestion* that a surprise attack on the city was a *way of getting even with the enemy* for the previous night's raid.

. . . .

3. After the funeral, the relatives and friends tried to appear in a *gay, holiday* mood, as if trying to *wipe out* their sadness for Aunt Helen's death.

. . . .

. . . .

4. The *unyielding* courage of the old general first showed itself when he was a young *student in military school.*

. . . .

. . . .

5. She *spoke out strongly against* the agreement with such *passionate intensity* that it was dropped.

. . . .

. . . .

6. His ignorance of these waters is *so deep it can hardly be measured,* so no one was surprised when he ran the boat onto a *sandbar just below the surface of the sea.*

. . . .

. . . .

7. A bad burn had *spoiled the looks of* one side of his face.

. . . .

. . . .

8. The bread was not *fit to be eaten,* and the butter was *so stale it had a sour taste.*

. . . .

9. The representative's supporters are so *loyal and faithful* to her that it is sometimes hard for them to *hold in check* their enthusiasm.

. . . .

. . . .

EXERCISE 23D

To form an adjective from the noun *abyss* (Word List 23), we change the final *s* to *m* and add the adjective suffix *-al*, giving us ABYSMAL. This is an irregular formation, but most adjectives are formed from nouns either by adding an adjective suffix or by replacing the noun suffix with an adjective suffix.

By using ten different adjective suffixes, change the nouns below into their adjectival forms. Underline each adjective suffix and check your answers in your dictionary.

1. ardor ( )

2. rancor ( )

3. critic ( )

4. tragedy ( )

5. pallor ( )

6. serpent ( )

7. boy ( )

8. disruption ( )

9. beast ( )

10. burden ( )

EXERCISE 23E

Write out, in the spaces provided, the words from Word List 23 for which a definition, homonym, synonym, or antonym is given on the next page. When you are asked to give a root or a prefix, you should refer back to the preceding exercise; the information you require will be found there. Make sure that each of your answers has the same number of letters as there are spaces. A definition followed by a number is a review word; the number gives the Word List from which it is taken.

If all the words are filled in correctly, the boxes running up and down the answer spaces will give the first seven words of a riddle. The riddle will be concluded in Exercise 24E.

1. an act that returns harm for harm

2. a synonym for *bottomless*

3. a synonym for *untiring* (22)

4. a shallow place caused by a sandbar

5. a synonym for *loving*

6. the inside parts of animals (6)

7. to be a sign of something that is to come

8. sour through having gone stale

9. to grow weaker or less (6)

10. a synonym for *suggest*

11. an antonym for *unleash*

12. an antonym for *apathy*

13. the main argument of a speech or piece of writing (5)

14. a student in a military school

15. blue-black (said of the skin) (5)

16. an antonym for *flawless*

17. made in layers pressed together (17)

18. still; not flowing (20)

19. to wipe out

20. rate of speed

21. slow (19)

22. ill at ease (21)

23. that can be eaten

24. an antonym for *gloomy*

25. to speak out against

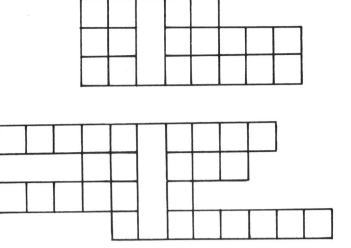

WORDLY WISE 23

In Britain ARDOR is spelled *ardour* and CURB (but only in the meaning of "a stone or concrete siding along each side of a street") is spelled *kerb*.

RANCID is pronounced *RAN-sid*.

When an army plundered the goods of its enemy, the enemy *retaliated* at least partly to take back what had been stolen. Such an act was called a REPRISAL, from the French *re-* (back) plus *pris* (take). *Reprisals* nowadays usually take the form of inflicting punishment on an enemy rather than recovering plundered goods.

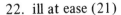

Word List 24

ARDUOUS	DUBIOUS	NICETY
AWKWARD	ENVISAGE	OFFICIOUS
BARRIER	EXERT	REGATTA
CHALET	MANSION	SKITTISH
DEVOID	MORON	VEER
DISGRUNTLED		

Look up the words above in your dictionary. Note that some of the words have more than one meaning. When you feel that you know *all* the meanings of *all* the words, go on to the exercise below.

EXERCISE 24A

From the four choices under each phrase or sentence, you are to mark the one that is closest in meaning to the word appearing in italics. When the same word appears more than once, you should note that it is being used in a different sense.

1. *devoid* of color
   (a) abundance (b) full (c) empty (d) purity

2. a *nicety* of judgment
   (a) very slight error (b) fine degree of accuracy (c) very great error (d) great improvement

3. We were *disgruntled*.
   (a) insulted (b) dissatisfied (c) uncomplaining (d) starving

4. an old *mansion*
   (a) large window with leaded frames (b) large, stately house (c) leather-covered bottle (d) winding staircase

5. a *chalet* in the mountains
   (a) steep-sided valley (b) snow-covered slope (c) cottage with overhanging roof (d) crude shelter for climbers

6. an *arduous* climb
   (a) dangerous (b) short (c) strenuous (d) easy

7. to *exert* an influence
   (a) be subject to (b) avoid (c) bring to bear (d) reject

8. the *barrier* across the road
   (a) white line (b) low bridge (c) telephone line (d) obstacle

135

9. to *veer* to the left
(a) point (b) swerve (c) be pushed (d) look

10. a *skittish* horse
(a) nervous (b) spotted (c) diseased (d) untamed

11. a *dubious* honor
(a) very great (b) unexpected (c) doubtful (d) well-deserved

12. We watched the *regatta.*
(a) car race (b) boat race (c) horse race (d) dog race

13. an *officious* person
(a) clever (b) important (c) hardworking (d) meddlesome

14. He is a *moron.*
(a) person of low intelligence (b) person from a foreign country (c) very religious person (d) easily-angered person

15. to *envisage* the scene
(a) be stunned by (b) imagine (c) look over (d) prepare

16. an *awkward* position
(a) difficult (b) reclining (c) relaxed (d) standing

17. an *awkward* child
(a) very tall (b) not clever (c) not graceful (d) very thin

Check your answers against the correct ones below. The answers are not in order; this is to prevent your eye catching sight of the correct ones before you have had a chance to do the exercise on your own.

10a. 16a. 5c. 12b. 4b. 15b. 9b. 1c. 11c. 13d. 7c. 17c. 6c. 2b. 14a. 8d. 3b.

Go back to your dictionary and look up again those words for which you gave incorrect answers. Only after doing this should you go on to the next exercise.

EXERCISE 24B
Each word from Word List 24 is used four times in the sentences below; one of the sentences in each group uses the word incorrectly. You are to circle the letter that precedes that sentence. Do not circle more than one letter in any one group.

1. (a) As the wind *veers*, you have to adjust the sail. (b) The boat *veered* into the wind. (c) The car keeps *veering* to the left because the steering is defective. (d) The length of the boards ought not to *veer* by more than two inches.

2. (a) He is completely *devoid* of ambition. (b) She was *devoided* of everything she owned. (c) Her speech was *devoid* of any references to the election. (d) He was a man utterly *devoid* of pity.

3. (a) She is too *awkward* with the needle to make her own clothes. (b) An *awkward* smell issued from the trash cans along the street. (c) He shifted his weight *awkwardly* from one foot to the other. (d) The steering is a little *awkward* on these old cars.

4. (a) "It's not fair," he *disgruntled.* (b) She seemed *disgruntled* at being left out. (c) Their *disgruntled* manner left no doubt of their feelings. (d) A few *disgruntled* voices were heard complaining.

5. (a) I hope you appreciate the *niceties* of a painting like this. (b) The waiter brought a tray of *niceties* for us. (c) She judged to a *nicety* the amount that was needed. (d) He was lacking in the *niceties* of social behavior.

6. (a) I was just sitting quietly when some *officious* person asked me what I wanted. (b) He bustled around *officiously*, asking all kinds of questions. (c) She said he wished to see me on *officious* business. (d) She questioned us in such an *officious* manner that I decided not to answer her.

7. (a) Every spring they leave for their *chalet* in the mountains. (b) They *chalet* during the summer in this little cottage. (c) Little *chalets* dotted the side of the mountain. (d) The overhanging roof of the *chalet* keeps the snow away from the sides.

8. (a) I don't know who won the *regatta*. (b) We are praying for fine weather for Saturday's *regatta*. (c) Many of these little coastal towns have a weekly *regatta* during the summer. (d) The two *regattas* were dead level as they crossed the finish line.

9. (a) The horse backed away *skittishly* as we approached. (b) She became quite *skittish* as the evening wore on. (c) We put a little *skittish* on at the variety show. (d) I tried to change my horse for one less *skittish*.

10. (a) We tried to *envisage* the scene as he described it. (b) His dark *envisage* and black beard gave him a frightening appearance. (c) She *envisaged* a single great country stretching from sea to sea. (d) I tried to *envisage* what the problem might be.

11. (a) Invitations to the ball went out to all the *mansions* in the county. (b) As soon as he took office, he moved into the governor's *mansion*. (c) Everyone from the owner of the grandest *mansion* to the dweller in the humblest cottage was there. (d) We can *mansion* the guests in the east wing.

12. (a) Plants grow very *dubiously* here because of the poor soil. (b) Her suggestions were of *dubious* value. (c) She looked *dubiously* at me when I told her the price. (d) I assured her it was quite safe, but she still seemed *dubious*.

13. (a) The tests we have made of her intelligence indicate that she is a *moron*. (b) He seemed very *moron*, so I asked him what was troubling him. (c) Only a *moron* would find this movie amusing. (d) His *moronic* attempts at humor did not go over very well.

14. (a) Picasso *exerted* an enormous influence on modern painting. (b) By *exerting* all our strength, we managed to move the boulder. (c) She *exerted* us to make an even greater effort in the future. (d) If he *exerted* himself, he would get better grades.

15. (a) A lack of education can be a real *barrier* to success. (b) The police will *barrier* sightseers from the disaster area. (c) The police set up a *barrier* across the road. (d) Many *barriers* were set in her way, but she overcame them all.

16. (a) After a life of *arduous* toil, he retired to the country. (b) You need to be very *arduous* to survive in this cold climate. (c) After an *arduous* climb, we reached the top of the mountain. (d) It is an *arduous* task that you have set yourself.

EXERCISE 24C

Rewrite each of the sentences below, replacing the italicized word or phrase with a word from Word List 24 and writing the word in the form that fits the rest of the sentence. Use each word only once. Write your answers in the spaces provided.

1. She seemed *very annoyed and unhappy* when you called her a *person of low intelligence*.

   . . . .

   . . . .

2. I am in an *uncomfortable* position since both sides in the dispute are asking me to *bring to bear* whatever influence I have on their behalf.

   . . . .

   . . . .

3. Removing the *obstacle that blocked our path* was a *tiring and difficult* task.

   . . . .

   . . . .

4. They spend their winters in this *large, stately house* and their summers in a *Swiss cottage with an overhanging roof* in the mountains.

. . . .

. . . .

5. He was such an *unpleasantly meddlesome* person that I thought I should teach him some of the *finer points* of correct behavior.

. . . .

. . . .

6. A horse that is so *easily frightened* is of *doubtful* value to a riding stable.

. . . .

. . . .

7. The *sports meeting at which boat races were held* was *totally lacking in any* of the excitement we had expected.

. . . .

. . . .

8. I was sure the road *took a sudden turn* just ahead, and I could *picture in my mind* the car ending up in the ditch.

. . . .

. . . .

EXERCISE 24D

This exercise reviews the material covered on word origins.

Give the meanings of the prefixes italicized in the following words. Put (L) for a Latin prefix, (G) for a Greek prefix.

1. *sub*jugate ( ) ( )

2. *super*ficial ( ) ( )

3. *ex*pletive ( ) ( )

4. *anti*septic ( ) ( )

5. *pan*demonium ( ) ( )

6. *a*byss ( ) ( )

7. *pre*monition ( ) ( )

8. *im*punity ( ) ( )

Give the meanings of the roots italicized in the words below. Put (L) for a Latin root, (G) for a Greek root.

9. a*byss* ( ) ( )

10. *soci*able ( ) ( )

11. *aqua*tic ( ) ( )

12. inter*min*able ( ) ( )

13. pre*mon*ition ( ) ( )

14. *tempo*rary ( ) ( )

15. com*prehend* ( ) ( )

16. *chrono*meter ( ) ( )

Complete the following statements.

17. There are . . . . grams in a kilogram.

18. The bicentenary of the Declaration of Independence took place in the year . . . .

19. . . . . was the eighth month of the Roman calendar.

20. A tripod is a stand that has . . . . legs.

21. The Pentagon in Washington is a building

138

with . . . . sides.

EXERCISE 24E

Write out, in the spaces provided, the words from Word List 24 for which a definition, homonym, synonym, or antonym is given below. When you are asked to give a root or a prefix, you should refer back to the preceding exercise; the information you require will be found there. Make sure that each of your answers has the same number of letters as there are spaces. A definition followed by a number is a review word; the number gives the Word List from which it is taken.

If all the words are filled in correctly, the boxes running up and down the answer spaces will conclude the riddle begun earlier.

1. a synonym for *swerve*

2. profits from an activity (18)

3. an antonym for *graceful*

4. an antonym for *full*

5. money or other items given to the poor (15)

6. a large, stately house

7. a synonym for *obstacle*

8. unyielding (23)

9. a synonym for *meddlesome*

10. to picture in the mind

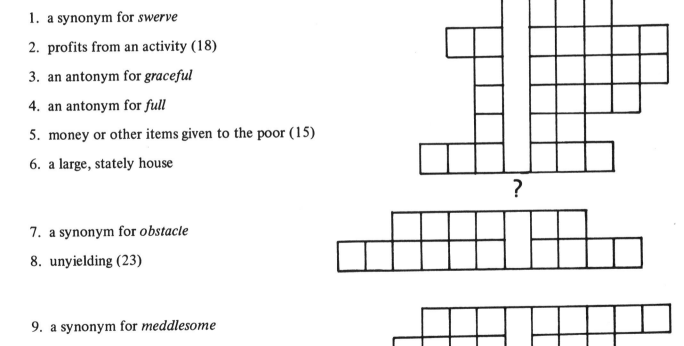

11. having to do with water (10)

12. an antonym for *contented*

13. a fine point or detail

14. an antonym for *easy*

15. nervous in a high-spirited way

16. dreadful (11)

17. a person of low intelligence

18. the mournful tolling of a bell (12)

19. a series of boat races

20. a synonym for *doubtful*

21. a Swiss cottage with overhanging roof

22. to bring to bear

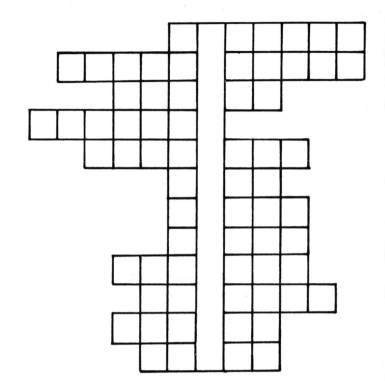

WORDLY WISE 24

CHALET is a Swiss-French word and is pronounced *sha-LAY*.

MORON comes from the Greek *moros* (foolish) and strictly speaking defines a person having a mental age of between 8 and 12. A moron is thus more intelligent than an *imbecile* (mental age between 3 and 7) and much more intelligent than an *idiot* (mental age below 3). All three terms are used loosely to describe a person who does something stupid or silly.

Official is an adjective meaning (1) of or having to do with an office, (2) coming from a person with authority, (3) suitable for an important officer or person. It may also be used as a noun meaning "a person holding an office, especially in government." Don't confuse this word with OFFICIOUS, which means "offering unwanted attention in a meddlesome manner."

ACROSS

1. dissatisfied and complaining
5. fast motion; swiftness
9. a large group of fish
10. fit to be eaten
12. to hold back; to check
14. untiring
16. to speak against strongly
18. to make an offer of marriage
20. a boat race
23. to rub out; to delete
25. a person of low intelligence
26. very loyal and loving
27. a strip of water running into the land
28. a distinctive trait or quality
32. a fairy-tale giant (17)
33. a student at a military school
34. easily frightened; nervous
36. to be a sign of future events
39. a wise and trusted adviser
40. bad smelling; bad tasting
42. to take by force
43. to bring to bear
44. money given to the poor (15)
45. an insult (3)
46. too deep to measure
47. something that blocks the way
48. to form a mental picture of
49. merry; gay

DOWN

1. having the looks spoiled
2. made of cheap material
3. a small detail; a fine point
4. to try hard; to strive
5. to change direction
6. to bring to an end
7. skill in dealing with people
8. questionable; doubtful
11. to roar; to shout out
13. a large, stately house
15. not real; imaginary
16. to eat greedily
17. a pretender to knowledge
19. saucy; bold (18)
21. a small wooden hammer used by judges
22. eagerness; enthusiasm
24. respect, mixed with wonder and fear (21)
27. that cannot be conquered
29. uncomfortable; clumsy
30. an act of retaliation
31. meddlesome
33. a Swiss cottage with overhanging roof
35. not given to talking
37. to search through thoroughly
38. requiring much effort; strenuous
41. totally lacking; empty
44. anything owned that has value (2)